BROAD STREET   *View from Green End.*

(Frontispiece)

PRESTEIGNE
PAST AND PRESENT

PRESTEIGNE
PAST AND PRESENT

By

W. H. HOWSE

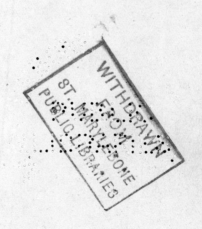

HEREFORD :

JAKEMANS LIMITED, 31, CHURCH STREET.

1945

No mirror aids our vision
When we would strive to tell
The story of our fathers,
How this or that befell.

We peer in dusty volumes
And read of feast and feud—
The jollity, the rancour,
Our reach and grasp elude.

Yet from the Past the Present,
And our reflective mind,
Within its human limits
May Past and Present bind.

The spell of night's soft footfall,
The dawn's first haunted hour,
A wistful strain of music,
The fragrance of a flower.

'Tis such can startle fancy,
Make sleeping shadows wake,
From some dark bourn emerging
Our solitude to break.

And thus we now adventure
To live in bygone days,
And linger with the pilgrims
On green, untrodden ways.

To hear again the voices
Of laughter or of scorn,
And touch the very texture
Of garments long outworn.

W.H.H.

CONTENTS.

ILLUSTRATIONS.

AUTHOR'S PREFACE

I have tried in this book to give the story of the Welsh border town of Presteigne from its earliest days to the present time. It is a story of a thousand years of ups and downs of fortune. In many ways it is a story of the Welsh border, and to make the narrative intelligible, I have had to introduce a background of both Welsh and English history. I have done this with as light a hand as possible, to avoid making the book appear like a "lesson book." At the same time I hope that the student of history (especially social history) will find enough in the narrative itself to make it a contribution of some value in that direction.

The book has not been written as a Guide to Presteigne, nor in any way as an advertisement, though it may be the means of bringing the little town and its surroundings to the notice of some people for the first time. Such readers may like to be told that it stands at 500 feet above sea level, and that its air is " fresh, bracing, and healthful " (to quote a local Guide). The latter fact goes almost without saying of any place in Radnorshire, and I can add my testimony that in no other town, in comparison with its population, have I seen so many *active* people over the age of 80.

I have written of the surrounding country at some length in the chapter entitled " Tales and Travels," for it is of a beauty and variety that would add lustre to any place, and calls for description. Enough has been said in the travel books about Presteigne as a motoring centre. I have added a map and a table of road distances, which may be helpful to motorists—as well as to those who are not quite certain where Presteigne is on the map.

One of my aims has been to get enough facts together to enable the reader to picture the place as it was at different periods —though such pictures are difficult of imagination, almost as difficult as trying to *hear* the full orchestra with only the symphony score in front of one. I realised this in talking to an old lady who left Presteigne in 1867, but remembered it more vividly than Canada, where she had since lived. The conditions which she described made up a picture which could have been imagined more easily by those who lived in the reign of Queen Anne than by the present generation. In other words, Presteigne and the border in 1867 had changed far less since, say, 1702 than they have since 1867.

There are so many little touches which the historian is apt to miss and which are required for painting the full picture. Horse travel, for instance, once so general in the country, as I have shown. As I write of it now, I have in mind how, only 50 years back, the old clockmaker of the town used to ride on his horse to the outlying farms to mend their grandfather clocks, and the doctor visited his patients on horseback. I have written of the fewer pleasure outings which farm servants had 50 or 60 years ago; I call to mind the fact that they lived in larger communities in those days, invariably living in the farm house, where often 12 or 15 sat down to every meal, and life was probably far from dull.

I add these two little touches as instances of what may be missed. I have tried, however, to include in the book a number of sidelights of this kind, to assist imagination. Readers of Kilvert's Diary will recognise in the picture of the 1870's conditions and ways of life very similar to those which he described for south Radnorshire.

I have to acknowledge my indebtedness to many who have kindly helped me in my work. There are very few of the older inhabitants of Presteigne whom I have not worried with my inquiries, and I have to thank one and all for their unfailing courtesy and help. Especially I have to thank Mr. H. Sawbridge for the photographs which he has taken for the book. I asked for a series which would show Presteigne as it actually is, without aiming at artistic effects, and he seems to me to have accomplished my aim, without sacrificing the latter. He has, moreover, made it a labour of love.

Among those outside Presteigne who have given me much valuable help and to whom I tender my thanks are: the Lord Lieutenant of Radnorshire (Sir Charles Venables-Llewelyn), who granted me access to the Shire Hall records; Professor William Rees, of Cardiff University; the Librarian of the National Library of Wales; Mr. George Marshall, Hon. Secretary of the Woolhope Club; the Rev. D. Stedman Davies, Hon. Secretary of the Radnorshire Society; Lt.-Col. G. Drage, D.S.O. (who gave me the run of his library). Nor would I forget Mr. F. C. Morgan and his staff at the Hereford City Library for their considerable help in my reference work; or Mr. E. J. Thurston, my publisher, for his many helpful suggestions.

W. H. HOWSE.

September, 1945.

PRESTEIGNE:
A PICTURE OF LIFE ON
THE WELSH BORDER

I

Introductory

" Duke " gave the writer his first memorable and lasting impression of Presteigne. Many travellers have recorded their impressions of the place, from Leland in 1540 to the R.A.C. Guide Book of 1940. Nearly all have had something good to say, each using the approved adjectives of his own time—beauteous, handsome, elegant, neat and well-built, respectable, delicious, comely and old-fashioned, charming, delightful, and the like.

There is still perhaps some measure of truth in all these adjectives. Duke, who had lived in Presteigne many years, described his own reactions to it in a leisureliness and a certain stateliness of movement, which one felt conveyed exactly the right idea.

" Duke," it should be explained, was a fine old carthorse, whose duties included the removal of the town's household rubbish each Tuesday and Friday morning. His cart lay at some distance from his stable,—so, while most people still lay abed (though the hour might be after 8), the empty streets echoed to his slow and heavy tread, as he was led from stable to cart. Seconds seemed to elapse between the time he planted first one foot, then another on the roadway. The nervous little old man who led him (a town character, since, alas, laid aside by illness) urged him on, but in vain and as one without hope. The hour was Duke's, and his measured footsteps the cadences of unhurried years.

Time indeed has laid a gentle hand on Presteigne. Few towns can have changed so little in the space of 400 years. At night it slumbers sound. It wakes to a day of dreamy quietude, which accords with the peace of the surrounding hills. Even on the Wednesday market-day it is possible to walk along Broad Street and High Street, the two main thoroughfares, and be unconscious of the fact that there is a market, so unobtrusive is it, hidden away down Back Lane. There is a certain liveliness from cattle and sheep being driven through the streets, but this is reduced to a minimum, since most of the animals arrive and depart in lorries.

What business exists is chiefly done in the High Street and the near-by part of Hereford Street, where are most of the shops and the two small Banks. How many times of an afternoon—in the evenings, too—is it possible to stand in those two streets and not see a soul! (save perhaps in the evenings for the inevitable loafers who gather round the butcher's shop at the top of Broad Street). For the town lies away from main roads, and lives, as it were, much on itself. It is this remoteness, this seclusion, which gives it a character of its own.

At the same time, the buildings are of a size and appearance which give reminder that here is a town where the Assizes have been held for 400 years, and the title of county town rests on old foundations. There is a dignity about the place which is lacking in many larger towns. You cannot get away from it, and after living in it for some time, you do not want to. It is like living with an old lady of compelling charm and irresistible manners.

We may, though, be permitted perhaps to smile at some of her artless pretensions. For what other county town of to-day has a street like Broad Street? There are cobble stones and quaint buildings in the other streets and—let it be specially mentioned—a curving vista of white cottages along Scottleton Street which forms a perfect picture of rural architecture of the 18th century. It is, moreover, possible to look down High Street and see the hills beyond. But, looking down Broad Street, for a moment one loses altogether the town-like impression in the beauty of the hill which fills the more distant view. Then one becomes conscious of a succession of old houses on both sides of the wide street, Georgian, Queen Anne, Jacobean, Tudor, with hardly a modern frontage save that of the Shire Hall—if we may call 1830 modern. At the bottom of the street there is the ancient recessed bridge over the Lugg, where one may stand and see the flash of the kingfisher's flight.

It is here in Broad Street that we get the true old-world charm of Presteigne—where there is hardly ever any traffic to disturb the wagtails and finches which play about the pavements, where only owls break the silence of the night, and where in summer-time is the continual darting to and fro of house-martins. Let it be added—there is a cowhouse in the very middle of our county town, and in this same street may be seen a leisurely procession of cows passing four times a day, by the Shire Hall itself, to and from their pastures beyond Lugg bridge.

Thus is Presteigne in the year of grace 1945. With a dwindling population, not much more than 1,100, its modern houses are few, and for the most part in two small groups, one at the entrance from Knighton, the other at the entrance from Kington.

In the town itself nearly all the shops and houses are old. Some have acquired Georgian or Victorian fronts, but behind show unexpected gables and timber-frame work of an earlier age. Others have hidden their stone and timber fronts under rough-cast or stucco. A few black-and-white buildings remain, among which the most notable is the Radnorshire Arms Hotel (which bears the date 1616). Fifty years ago many houses had their old tile roofs, but only a few of these are left. There are still some thatched cottages in and around Scottleton Street. And the solid stone walls of private gardens remain,—so high some of them that people have mistaken them for defensive walls—their grey-brown colour mellowed by the years, which have endowed them with a profusion of gilly flowers, valerian, arabis, ferns, and the like, to fit them into the general picture.

The casual visitor must take the interiors of the houses for granted. This is a pity, because so many of them have preserved that intimacy with the past which is of the very essence of the place: beautiful oak staircases, graceful mantelpieces, wainscotted rooms, ornamental panelling, broad-boarded floors, moulded ceiling beams—these are as their builders left them, solid and enduring. A quaint feature of some of the houses is a lack of passage space, one room opening into another. Walls of wattle and daub are also not uncommon.

This little picture of Presteigne, its rural quietude and its quaintness, is given here, because in a book which is intended to be both a history and an up-to-date account of the town, the setting of the story is apt to be lost in the story itself. To some people, perhaps rightly, the atmosphere of the place—its soul, so to speak—is more important than mere externals. To the writer, at any rate, it appears as essential to record that in the spring and summer-time bird song may be heard in whatever part of the town a person stands (thanks to the gardens on which every street backs), that goldcrests flit around the railway station, and that the mew of a buzzard overhead is a familiar sound, as to say that there are a beautiful church and less beautiful Assembly Rooms.

At a conference of British archæologists in 1943 a speaker urged that there should be a more realistic series of books about British towns, in which history gave way to conditions as they existed to-day. " If in your town," he said, " one of the most important buildings happens to be the office of the gas works, record the fact." Photographs have been added to this book, with the special object of showing Presteigne as it is now.

Ten years hence the picture may be very different. Change is inevitable. The best we can hope is that the changes may be planned, under a competent hand, with real care and understanding, and with some regard to the present character of the town,— so that, when another book comes to be written about Presteigne, and the changes are duly recorded, they may not appear as the ravages of Hunnish men, but rather the completion of work well begun, by those who valued their inheritance. So may the old lady of our metaphor still hold the destiny of the town, and the shade of Duke take no offence!

II

Before the Conquest

The original name of Presteigne was Presthemede. How this name gradually changed into the present name is told in a later chapter. Presthemede is Old English, and points to an origin when the Mercians or Saxons overran the surrounding district, before the Norman invaders arrived. The same applies to practically all the other places in Radnorshire near Presteigne, e.g., Radnor, Knighton, Norton, Cascob, Burlingjobb (pronounced Birchop). Even Discoed, though it sounds Welsh, appears to have an English origin, since it is described in the Domesday Book of 1086 as Discote. The other places are all mentioned in Domesday (though spelt differently), but not Presteigne. This has given rise to a doubt whether Presteigne existed before the Norman Conquest. Against this we have the fact of its old English name, and also the important fact that a part of the parish church has been identified as Saxon.

There are other omissions from Domesday which are hard to explain. In the case of Presteigne, there may be an explanation in the name itself. All authorities agree that the Prest part of the name comes from the old English "preost," which means "priest." While other writers have thought that the second part of the name is derived from "maed," meaning "meadow" (B. G. Charles suggests "hem maed" as meaning the border meadow), Professor Ekwall, in the Oxford Dictionary of English Place Names (1936), says that it comes from "haemed," meaning "household," and that the name means "the household of priests" (preosta haemed).*

The ecclesiastical parish of Presteigne is a very large one (over 11,000 acres), and it seems likely that there was here by the Lugg stream, well stocked with fish, a colony or college of clergy who served the large district of which it was a centre. Probably there was little more than the church and "the household." When we come to Gruffydd and his destructive visit to the neighbourhood in 1052, we shall see how easily such a community might totally have disappeared for a time, to leave no record for Domesday. The church and whatever settlement was around it might have been

---

* There is only one other place in Wales with the prefix "Prest" to its name: this is Prestatyn, originally Preston (priest's town).

attached to the manor of Clatertune, which is mentioned in Domesday as having two hides, and is believed to have lain around Clatterbrook bridge, on the south-east side of the town.

In passing, it might be mentioned that in a history of Clun, in Shropshire, it is stated that there was originally at Clun a college or brotherhood of priests, who took it in turn to visit the outlying chapels for services. The parish of Clun was even larger than that of Presteigne—over 20,000 acres. The college is believed to have been started about the year 900. That at Presteigne may have been of earlier date, since the Mercians were firmly established in the district long before 900.

The Welsh name for Presteigne is Llanandras, Andras standing for Andrew. Presteigne church is dedicated to St. Andrew. We do not know the original dedication. St. Andrew is probably a Norman dedication. Their churches were invariably dedicated to a saint of the Roman Church, and they often changed the dedications of churches in conquered Welsh territory. They even re-dedicated St. David's Cathedral to St. Andrew. It is probable, therefore, that Presteigne got its Welsh name of Llanandras after its occupation by the Normans. It may well be that the Welsh name did not arise until much later—until, in fact, the time when Welshmen first felt it safe to settle in the neighbourhood. It may have been Welsh settlers of this later period who changed Discote into Discoed. Kitchin's map of about 1750 gives the name as Discot

Practically the only old Welsh name preserved in Presteigne is that of its river. Many rivers and streams have kept their ancient names, despite conquests and invasions by alien races. The Lugg has shortened its Celtic name, but not beyond recognition. The ancient name was Llugwy, which means " the bright stream." There was formerly a house by the river near Mynachty called Glan Llugwy (on the bank of the Llugwy).

No traces of very early Man have been found in the immediate neighbourhood of Presteigne. Some relics of the Bronze Age (going back, say, 3,500 years) have been brought to light around Knighton, but none at Presteigne.* There are no earthworks of Roman origin in the neighbourhood (although Roman coins have been unearthed at Shobdon), but there was an important Roman road eight miles away, Watling Street, which connected Chester with Monmouth, and ran through Leintwardine, Wigmore, Aymestry, and Kenchester. Nearer at hand, on Wapley and Burfa Hills,

---

* There are cultivation terraces (lynchets), probably of this Age, at Lingen, and tumuli near Walton and on Radnor Forest. The Four Stones and other standing stones near Walton may be earlier.

STAPLETON CASTLE — *Ruins on early Norman motte.*

OFFA'S DYKE — *English side near Yew Tree Farm.*

(To face page 160.)

COLE'S HILL   *View from Folly Farm.*

SILIA COTTAGE   *The Warden in background.*

(*To face page* 17).

are extensive traces of two of the largest British " camps " on the Border. To both is assigned an earlier date than that when the Romans first came to Wales—probably 100 or 200 B.C.

Sir Cyril Fox has said that in Wales, as in Ireland, there is a folk-memory binding the remote past with the present, and quotes some striking examples. A tradition has been handed down from ancient times that Caractacus spent the last days of his freedom in this country on Wapley Hill, among the Ordovices, who inhabited this part of the country. It is said that, when he left the camp, he split his forces into two, one moving over the hills towards Knighton, the other following first the valley of the Lugg, both forces making for a rendezvous by the valley of the Teme, to be ultimately defeated by the Romans in A.D. 51.

Mention of the Ordovices reminds us that this Brythonic tribe occupied the country which now comprises the counties of Radnor and Montgomery, with the adjacent portions of Merionethshire and Denbighshire. Historians agree that they were the first Welsh-speaking Celts to arrive in Wales. After the Romans left Britain they spread into South Wales and conquered the people of Goidelic and Iberian stock who had settled there. It is strange to reflect that in Radnorshire, where Welsh is no longer spoken, the language was spoken earlier than in most parts of Wales, and that folk from Radnorshire taught a large part of Wales the Welsh language.

After the Romans left Wales (about 400 A.D.), and Brythons from the Solway and Clyde had occupied North Wales (while the Ordovices spread south), the country gradually settled into three main divisions—Gwynedd in the north, Deheubarth in the south, and Powys between the other two. Presteigne has little to do with Welsh history, so we need not concern ourselves about the wars which were constantly going on between the rulers of these three realms, and the great warriors who were sometimes able, by force of arms, to weld all Wales into one to fight the Mercians, Saxons, Danes, etc., who invaded the country, and later the Normans and English.

Presteigne and the country around, including Kington, are believed originally to have been in Powys, but afterwards they formed part of another division known as Rhwng Gwy a Hafren (between the Wye and the Severn), which took in modern Radnor-shire and a few districts outside. It is thought that the castle site known as the Warden, which overlooks the town, was used at this period as a look-out station against the Mercians,* and that Castle Ring, near Evenjobb, is a Welsh " camp " of the same period.

---

* J. G. Wood, Woolhope Transactions, 1912.

The midland kingdom of Mercia soon spread its conquests into this neighbourhood under King Penda (626-655), and before the year 700 the whole district from Knighton to Old Radnor was in Mercian hands. By about 785 King Offa had completed his famous Dyke, which marked the boundary beyond which no Welshman might pass with safety. The Dyke passes three miles to the west of Presteigne, which it thus left in Mercia. It lies to the east of Kington and Old Radnor, but these and a few other places on the other side of the Dyke remained in English occupation.

With the decline of the Mercian power, the Welsh began raiding the border. Then came more terrible foes, the Danes. King Edward the Elder (son of Alfred the Great) built Wigmore Castle in 921 in an effort to stop the Danes and the Welsh, but for 100 years this part of the border was at the mercy of one or other of these raiders. Some kind of peace came with Edward the Confessor on the English throne, but it meant more foreigners. This time they were Normans, whom Edward, son of a Norman mother, introduced into the neighbourhood.

Edward himself had a " castle " at Womaston, near Walton, of which the mound may still be seen. Kington is said to take its name from him. Other Saxons came into the neighbourhood, or were already established here. The Norman lord was Osbern, son of Richard " the Scrub," who lived at Richard's Castle. His territory stretched as far as Titley, according to Domesday, and must have included Presteigne, with the other places which it mentions as belonging to him—Discoed, Cascob, Knill, Little Brampton, Kinnerton, etc.

So we come to the first great Welsh warrior who penetrated into Radnor territory. This was Gruffydd ap Llywelyn (ap means " son of "), who was as formidable as his name. He came from Gwynedd, and made himself master of Powys and Deheubarth. He also scored a great victory over the Mercians. Then, after attacking Edward's Normans and Saxons in 1052 and beating them in a big battle near Leominster, he laid waste the border, and destroyed most of anything left over by previous raiders. An old historian said the district did not recover for 30 years. Another historian says that, as a result of this visit and the previous Danish raids, " ruins occupied the sites of what had been flourishing towns; churches, monasteries, and even castles had been destroyed." It is quite probable that at this period Presteigne temporarily disappeared. Domesday's comment in 1086 on most of the neighbouring manors which it mentions is " Was and is waste."

Gruffydd returned to the border in 1055, sacked Hereford, and killed the bishop, sheriff and other notables whom he captured.

The local guide book story that he killed these people at Presteigne loses sight of the fact that history records they were killed at Glasbury. Soon afterwards the famous Harold took a hand in affairs. He led a successful campaign against the Welsh, and eventually in 1063 Gruffydd was betrayed and killed by his own people. Harold, before he left Wales, built the first castle at New Radnor.

Harold then met his death at the battle of Hastings, and soon the Normans of William the Conquerer arrived on the Welsh border. Thus entered the Lords Marchers, who ruled a large part of Wales (with occasional set-backs from the Welsh) for over 450 years.

III

The Lords Marchers

William the Conqueror's plan for the conquest of Wales was simple and convenient. He sent to the border some of his greatest warriors, with his free permission to take as much Welsh territory as they could lay their hands on, on the understanding that they could keep what they won. It was a convenient plan, because it cost him nothing, made a handsome return for services rendered, and got rid of some turbulent barons. Moreover, the Lords Marchers, as they were called, had to keep the March* in a sufficient state of defence to prevent the Welsh from making inroads into English territory. The Marchers, in return, were allowed to take over the same powers as the Welsh rulers formerly held whose territory they stole, and enjoyed nearly all the rights of a king. They had their own sheriffs and courts, with power of life and death over their own people, and the English king's writ did not run in the land they ruled. It was not until the time of Henry VIII that they finally lost these powers.

There were three great Lord Marcher families connected with the early history of Presteigne and its neighbourhood after the Norman Conquest. We have already mentioned the family of Richard the Scrub at Richard's Castle. They changed their name to de Say (hence Stokesay) later, and held Stapleton castle and the lordship of Stapleton until the early part of the 13th century. Then Ralph Mortimer got possession of Wigmore Castle in 1074 and began that career of conquest which his successors at Wigmore continued, to make their family eventually rulers of a large part of the border and Radnor lands.

The third family was that of the de Bohuns, lords of Hereford from 1200 to 1373. To the de Bohuns went the lordship of Huntington (as well as many other lordships). Their importance to us is that Presteigne was included in the lordship of Huntington. It could not have had better connections, for of all the great lords of England, the de Bohun family probably deserved best the name of noble. With Huntington, which included Kington as well as Presteigne, went the lordships of Brecknock and Hay, and these three lordships, once part of the vast territories of the de Braose

---

* From the Saxon word "mearc," meaning "boundary."

family, remained in the possession of the de Bohuns and their successors the Stafford family until 1521 (when they passed to the Crown).

And now a word about castles, including that of Presteigne. Castle " tumps " abound on the border, and nowhere more than in Radnorshire. The great majority of the mounds were probably thrown up in the early days of the Conquest, and the " castles " erected on them were originally no more than wooden towers, protected by palisades, which in many cases enclosed a courtyard containing the tower. Presteigne was of this courtyard (motte and bailey) type, which is seen to perfection in the site of Crug Eryr, a mile above the Forest Inn on the other side of Radnor Forest. These wooden structures served the Normans, who built them as temporary outposts and defences against the Welsh. Later many of them, but not all, were replaced by stone buildings.

The sites chosen for these more formidable castles were carefully selected from those already occupied, the rest being discarded. Thus around Presteigne there are several castle mounds which were probably only occupied for a short time and never had a stone castle—the mounds, for instance, at Evenjobb, Kinnerton, Discoed, Staunton-on-Arrow. Presteigne and Stapleton, on the other hand, were considered important enough to have stone defences. Both were probably built not later than, say, 1160.

The following were Norman castles on this part of the border: Wigmore, Huntington, Richard's Castle, Eardisley, Lynhales (Lyonshall), New Radnor, Presteigne, Stapleton, Norton, Knighton, Knucklas, and Bleddfa.* Of these the most important were Wigmore (which became one of the largest in England), Huntington, Eardisley (the home of the Baskervilles for centuries), and New Radnor. All in the present county of Radnor eventually came into the possession of the Mortimers. Exactly when they got Presteigne is not recorded, but it was almost certainly in the first half of the 13th century, soon after the de Bohuns acquired the lordship of Huntington by marriage with a de Braose, the Mortimers holding Presteigne from the de Bohuns. Eardisley was conveyed by the de Bohuns to the Baskervilles in 1252.

A younger son of the Mortimers married the heiress of Richard's Castle about 1210, and thus became lord of Richard's Castle and Stapleton, the two lordships being under one ownership. With

---

* The only *stonework* remains of any account to be seen to-day are at Wigmore (fairly considerable), Lyonshall, and Huntington (the ruins at Stapleton not belonging to the original castle). The stones of Knucklas castle are incorporated in the Knucklas railway viaduct.

Stapleton went Lugharness, a lordship which took in some districts
south and south-east of Presteigne, extending as far as Titley, and
also included some detached parts of Herefordshire west of Presteigne, towards Cascob.* The lordships of Huntington and Stapleton were both reckoned as part of Herefordshire,† which placed
Presteigne definitely in England, though under Lord Marcher rule,
and outside the jurisdiction of the sheriff of the county.

All this time Presteigne was a very small place, of no account
apart from its castle. It happened, however, to lie at important
cross-roads, one from Leominster, which branched at Presteigne to
New Radnor in one direction, and to Rhayader (through Discoed
and Cascob) in another, and the other road from Hereford, over
Lugg Bridge and Stonewall Hill to Knighton, Montgomery, etc.
The road to New Radnor lay by way of Green End and the Slough
to Beggar's Bush and Kinnerton. There is a fork in this old track,
about three-quarters of a mile past Cold Oak, which leads down
into Evenjobb. There was another important road or track used
until the 18th century, which proceeded through Walton and Old
Radnor to Gladestry and Painscastle. There was also the road,
less important than now, which connected Presteigne with Whitton
and Pilleth; this road proceeded to Llangunllo. Kington, too, was
connected with Presteigne by another road, through Titley.

What chapters could be written of the many famous people
who must have journeyed through the village! The Mortimers,
riding from Wigmore through Lingen and Stapleton, would constantly have to pass through on their way to and from their Welsh
castles of New Radnor‡ and Cefnllys. Kings and their armies
passed this way, too, on their journeys from or into Wales; Henry
II, for instance, on his way back to England through New Radnor
and Leominster in 1163, and John, hurrying from Leominster in
1216 to attack New Radnor castle.

King John, according to tradition, had a hunting lodge at Barland, which he used when staying at Ludlow or Leominster. His
journeys there would lie through Presteigne and along the old road
to Evenjobb.

To return to our history—as we saw in the first chapter, Wales
was divided into realms, whose leaders were constantly quarrelling.
This was a great handicap to those who wished to defend their
country against the inroads of the Lords Marchers. They were
helped, however, by the fact that in England also, until the battle

---

* Owen's Pembrokeshire.
† Victoria History of Herefordshire.
‡ Originally a de Braose possession, but acquired by the Mortimers
  through marriage with a de Braose heiress about 1235.

of Evesham in 1265, there was often warfare between the king and some of his leading barons. The Welsh princes were clever enough to take advantage of this, and allied themselves with either the king or the barons, as best suited their purpose. This is a broad picture of Welsh history for 200 years after the Conquest.

There were many " three-corner " contests as well, and much changing of sides, into which we need not enter. Evesham broke the power of the barons and, without allies, the Welsh were not strong enough to continue the struggle.

If Presteigne did not see the Welsh prince, Rhys ab Gruffydd, who allied himself with Henry II against the barons and was often on the border, it almost certainly saw the army which Roger Mortimer and Hugh de Say (of Richard's Castle) took against him in 1195, to meet defeat at New Radnor; and it undoubtedly had a visit from the next great Welsh prince to reach the border, Llywelyn ap Iorwerth (Llywelyn the Great), who found allies in many of the barons against King John. Since the Mortimers and their friends opposed him, Llywelyn overran much of their territory in 1212, taking Presteigne and Knighton castles, among others.

Llywelyn later became a signatory of Magna Carta, but made his peace with Henry III. Then the execution of some Welsh prisoners by the English in 1231 brought him to the border again, and into the neighbourhood of Presteigne, on a raid of reprisals, when the Welsh army " committed the most frightful ravages, burning even the churches and monasteries, and in them several noble ladies and young maidens who had taken refuge there."*

Presumably Presteigne castle survived this attack. But its end came soon afterwards, for in 1262 the last Llywelyn (ap Gruffydd) " reduced the castles of Bleddfa, Knucklas, Knighton, Norton, and Presteigne."† The " reduction " as far as Presteigne was concerned (and probably Norton too) appears to have been an entire cancellation, for we hear no more of the castle. In the map by Professor William Rees, of South Wales and the Border in the Fourteenth Century, the site is marked as the " Casteldiche."

As everyone knows, Llywelyn was killed near Builth in 1282. Edmund Mortimer of Wigmore was one of the English leaders who brought about his end. There is a local tradition, which can be traced back to at least the 18th century, that the occupant of Stapleton castle also played a leading part in Llywelyn's death. There is no historical evidence, however, to support the story which has somehow got about that his name was Elias Walwyn. The writer

---

* Wright's History of Ludlow and the Welsh Border.
† J. E. Lloyd's History of Wales.

has seen a book of about 1810 which mentions the name Walwyn as one of those present, but describes that individual as a Hay man; this is probably right, since the Walwyns settled at Hay in the reign of William the Conqueror. Even more conclusive, Leland, writing about 1540, said he saw at Hay "the ruins of a gentleman's place called Waulwin be whose means prince Lluelin was sodenli taken at Builth Castle."

IV

Peace and War

After the death of the last Llywelyn, the power of the Lords Marchers became more confined. Edward I lost little time in bringing what was known as the Principality of Wales under the English Crown, leaving the Lords Marchers in possession of the territories they had already won, which they continued to govern as before. With no fresh fields to conquer, they settled down to a certain amount of fighting amongst themselves, and protecting what they had already won from the inroads of the Welsh. On the whole the Welsh kept fairly quiet, though twice Edward III, who did not particularly trust them, gave orders for the border castles to be put into a state of good defence—Stapleton probably among others. Edward I had already found employment for his new Welsh subjects at the battle of Falkirk, which was won largely by his Welsh archers.

Edward III found the Welsh archers equally useful in his French and Scottish wars. This part of the border was famous for its bowmen, who fought under local leaders at Crecy, Poictiers, and Agincourt. One of these leaders was Sir John Cornewall, whose family had inherited Stapleton before the end of the 14th century, and also possessed Downton, near New Radnor; he took to Agincourt 30 men-at-arms and 90 archers.

With some degree of peacefulness restored in the 14th century, the pastoral life of the people began to flourish, sheep-raising being the principal industry. The scarcity of labour caused by the Black Death in 1349 led the Mortimers to let some of their lands to tenant farmers. It is possible that at this period Welshmen settled around Presteigne. A sign that Presteigne was growing is that the church appears to have been rebuilt and enlarged about this time. Williams, in his history of Radnorshire, mentions extensions to the church by one of the Mortimers. It seems probable that this was Roger Mortimer, the first Earl of March, who was later executed by Edward III.

The Mortimers continued to hold Presteigne during the 14th century, but the lordship of Huntington, in which it was included, changed hands in 1373, when the last de Bohun, Earl of Hereford, died; it passed by marriage to the Earls of Stafford, who later became Dukes of Buckingham. With the attainder and execution of the third Duke in 1521, the family possessions passed into the hands of the Crown.*

After the close of the 14th century Presteigne and the border soon again became involved in warfare. Owen Glendower is the darling of Welsh history. Yet Wales has little for which to thank him. He accomplished about as much destruction in the country as did the two Cromwells in England, and with more serious results to his countrymen, despite his patriotism and enlightened ideas. The arrival of his forces in Radnor territory was signalled by the destruction of New Radnor castle and town, following which event Presteigne itself was attacked and burnt.† This happened in 1401.

Next year Glendower totally defeated an English force under the command of Edmund Mortimer, uncle of the young Earl of March, in a battle fought at Pilleth (sometimes known as the battle of Bryn Glas), having destroyed the castles of Knucklas and Knighton before meeting Mortimer. He took Edmund prisoner.

There seems some doubt about the behaviour of the border men whom Edmund took to this battle: a number are reported to have gone over to the Welsh side. Edmund, whom Henry IV refused to ransom, did the same later, and called on the men of New Radnor and Presteigne to support Glendower, and put their young lord, then in Henry's custody, on the English throne, as the lawful successor to Richard II. He completed his alliance with Glendower by marrying a daughter of the latter.

The growing power of Glendower's rebellion caused Henry in 1403 to give instructions for strengthening the defences of various border castles. Among those named in his order were Richard's Castle (under Sir Thomas Talbot), Huntington (under the Countess of Stafford), Lyonshall (under Lord Fitz Walter), Eardisley, and Stapleton. The last-named was under the command of Richard Cornewall.

---

* This would mean that the lordship of Huntington, including Presteigne, became a Crown possession. The Mortimer possessions, including all their Radnor lands, also became Crown property when Edward IV was made king (see later in this chapter). According to Jones's History of Brecknockshire, a Survey of the possessions of the Duke of Buckingham taken in 1522 showed that Edmund, the last of the Mortimers, held two knights' fees at Presteigne. It does not seem, therefore, as if the Mortimers ever held Presteigne as overlords, though they probably worked the manor with their own lordships. The manor remained a Crown manor up to modern times, being governed by a steward, who was usually of noble rank and who appointed a deputy.

† An Inquisitio post Mortem of 1402 said of certain rents due from Presteigne that they " are of no value beyond reprise because the tenements are destroyed and burnt by the enemies and rebels of the King."

It is interesting to read about the king's concern for Stapleton, because Richard Cornewall's successor, John Cornewall of Stapleton (already mentioned above) married the king's sister, Elizabeth. Henry IV and the young Prince Henry were several times on the border in their campaigns against the Welsh, and it seems more than likely that we can add their names to the list of famous visitors to this neighbourhood.

Glendower does not seem to have troubled this part of the border again, and his rebellion ceased to be of much account after 1408. But the effects of the ravages he committed were felt for many a long year. Repressive laws were passed against Welshmen, and many were turned adrift as the result of the wholesale destruction of town and manor alike.

Presteigne again came into the war news with the outbreak of the Wars of the Roses. It naturally stood for the White Rose and the House of York, since the Duke of York, who claimed the throne, had inherited the Mortimer estates from his mother, Anne Mortimer, on the death in 1424 of her brother, the last male of the long line of Mortimer. The duke was killed at Wakefield, but his son, the young Earl of March, with an army largely drawn from his Radnor and Herefordshire lordships, won a decisive battle in 1461 against the Lancastrians at Mortimer's Cross (between Aymestrey and Kingsland), and so became Edward IV.

The Lancastrian Army on their way to this battle are said to have passed through Presteigne. History records the desperate flight of those who survived the battle, over Shobdon marshes, through Kinsham woods, and through Presteigne again, in an effort to get away from the Yorkist country—a flight in which many fell by the way at the hands of the local people, who hunted and killed without mercy.

The further battles of the Roses do not concern us, beyond the fact that men from these parts continued to fight on the Yorkist side, and a number laid down their lives at Bosworth, where Richard III fell, last of the House of York—among them Walter Devereux of Weobley, first Lord Ferrers of Chartley.* It is perhaps worth recalling, in this connection, that there was formerly an inn at Presteigne called the Blue Boar, which was the cognisance of Richard III.

The two wars, Glendower's and the Roses, left the whole border in a state of excitement and unrest. The woods became infested with bands of outlaws and robbers. The arrow slits in

---

* The arms of this family formerly appeared on one of the buttresses of the south aisle in Presteigne church.

Presteigne church tower were probably not there for mere ornament. The bandits, Welsh and English alike, descended on the countryside and made a practice of seizing some of the leading inhabitants, to hold them to ransom. Acts were passed, making it high treason for Welshmen to carry off Englishmen into Wales, but not with much effect. As late as 1534 there was an Act to punish severely Welshmen who attempted " any assaults or affrays " on the inhabitants of the counties of Hereford, Gloucester and Salop. How these conditions were improved, and the man who did it, will be shown in the next chapter.

There was another and more peaceable class of refugee for whom the wild country of these parts provided sanctuary. This consisted of the victims of religious persecution, the Lollards in particular, of Henry IV's and Henry V's reigns. Sir John Oldcastle (later Lord Cobham), one of the principal Lollards, was a native of Almeley, and hid for several years around Deerfold and Radnor Forests. Chapel Farm, near Wigmore, is said to have been one of his hiding-places.

V

Two Bishops

In this chapter we shall see how one bishop gave Presteigne prosperity, and another peace. The first bishop was Richard Martin, who was a native of Presteigne and became bishop of St. David's in 1482. Apparently he died soon after being made bishop, and he was succeeded by another in 1483. He was probably a personal acquaintance of Edward IV, coming from the same neighbourhood, and had acted as the king's ambassador on important missions abroad. It was he who obtained for Presteigne, doubtless through his influence with the king (who would know Presteigne well) the privilege of a weekly market and two annual fairs.

The effect was very soon felt, as we shall see from what Leland said about it (quoted below). It changed Presteigne into a sizeable town, later to become for many years the largest in what is now Radnorshire. The date of the change we do not know precisely, but it probably happened in the period 1470-80, before Martin was made bishop. Again we may take the church for our guide, for soon after this period it was once more extended by the construction of the present beautiful chancel and south aisle.

Before repeating what Leland said about the change, it would perhaps be as well to point out an error made by Lewis in his Topographical Dictionary of 1845 and repeated in some recent books, even in the Encyclopædia Britannica. These all name the bishop benefactor as David Martin, who was Bishop of St. David's 1296-1328. He had no connection with Presteigne.

Leland, who made his celebrated tour through England and Wales in 1533-45, wrote:—

(1) There is a 2 miles upperward a stone bridge over Lug at Presteine, which town of Presteine was endowed of late yeres with priviledges and a market by the intercession of Rich. Martin, Bysshope of St. Davyd's, and before Chancellor of the Marches, embassadour into Spaine and other strange countries.

(2) Presteine was but a Walsche village about Kynge Edward the 4 tyme, untyll Rich. Martyn, Bysshope of St. Davyd's and Chancellor of the Marches, got priviledges for it, and made it a market toune, that now is very celebrate for corne.

We might also hear what Camden, another traveller, who wrote about 1585, has to say of Presteigne's sudden rise to fame:—

> Prestaine, in British Llan Andre, that is St. Andrew's Church, which of a very little village within the memory of our grandfathers, is by the means of Richard Martin, Bishop of St. David's, grown now to be so great a mercate Town and Faire withall, that at this day it dammereth and dimmeth the light in some sort of Radnor.

The next bishop who helped Presteigne was a very different kind of man. Neither did he come exactly in the guise of a fairy godmother. Something was said in the last chapter about the lawless condition which existed on the border in the 15th century. Matters did not improve much even after Henry VIII came to the throne. So the Court of the Council of Wales and the Marches was formed to administer justice in the Marches and put down disorder. It had a lord president, who resided at Ludlow, and down to the outbreak of the Civil War was the chief instrument of government in Wales. The Court was finally abolished in 1689.

One of its first presidents was Roland Lee, Bishop of Lichfield. Lee was just the man for the task. He had helped the king in his divorce and had married him to Anne Boleyn, receiving his bishopric as a reward. Utterly fearless, and loyal to the king, he set about his appointed work with an enthusiasm and ruthlessness which thoroughly upset the calculations of the bandits and murderers who had held so much of Wales at their mercy. He hung them by batches in every town he passed through, and if one of them was killed before his trial, his body was put in a sack and hanged with the rest.

His correspondence with Thomas Cromwell, the king's minister, about his work has been preserved. This is what he says about Presteigne, in a letter written in 1535:

> I have been into Wales at Presteyne, where I was right heartilie welcomed with all the honest of that parte, as Sir James Baskerville and many other, without any speares or other fashion as heretofore hath been used, as at large this bearer shall enforme you; which journey was thought muche dangerouse to some, but, God willing, I entend after Easter to lye one month at Presteyne, even among the thickest of the theves, to doo my master suche service as the strongest of them all shall be affrayed to doo as to fore, God willing.

Not a very flattering picture of Presteigne, but doubtless matters improved after Lee's visit, as they did elsewhere on the border, which began to enjoy a feeling of peace and security it had not known for many years. People spoke of the period as " Bishop

Roland's justice." Lee laid a heavy hand on the gipsies, only recently established in this country. He it was, too, who made Welshmen shorten their names by cutting out the abs and aps.

An important series of Acts was passed while Lee was in office, which brought about the final union of England and Wales. The principal Act, passed in 1535, did away with the Marcher Lordships, and created five new counties, namely, Denbighshire, Montgomeryshire, Radnorshire, Brecknockshire, and Monmouthshire, and for the first time fixed the boundary between England and Wales.

The new county of Radnor was made up chiefly from the old Welsh commote known as Gwerthrynion (in the west), and the "cantrefs" of Elfael (south), and Maelienydd (north, centre and east), with the separate border lordships such as Presteigne, Radnor and Knighton. Presteigne became the easternmost town in the new county, and also in Wales (hence the saying from St. David's to Presteigne), the boundary with Herefordshire being half-way across the Lugg bridge at the bottom of Broad Street. New Radnor was made the county town, though it was probably smaller than Presteigne even in 1536, when the Act came into force.

The new legislation also set up Courts of Great Sessions, with their own circuits of judges. These lasted until 1830, when the Assizes took their place, within the English circuit system. In Radnorshire the Great Sessions were to be held alternately at Rhayader and New Radnor, but the judge who went to Rhayader was murdered almost at the first Sessions to be held there, and an Act of 1542 laid down that the Sessions should be held alternately at New Radnor and Presteigne, " and never from henceforth to be kept or holden at Rhayader."

So Presteigne got a good name at last—at any rate, a better name than Bishop Lee gave it. It is open to doubt whether the Great Sessions were ever held at New Radnor, though this had been made the county town. They appear to have gone to Knighton occasionally in the 17th century, but they were usually held at Presteigne from 1542 to 1830, and this has been the Assize town for the county since 1830.

VI

Struggle and Stress

The border gained a peace and security under Henry VIII which it had not known for long centuries. Probably at this time there was a fresh inflow of Welsh people into Presteigne, whose market was largely attended, and soon drew much of New Radnor's trade. From an Act passed in 1544 it would look as if its rapid rise had led to a certain amount of " jerry building." The Act, which mentioned other towns as well, ran as follows:

> Forasmuch as in tymes past diverse and many beautifulle houses of habitation have been within the walles and liberties of (here followed a list of the towns, 23 altogether), which now are fallen down and decayed, and at this time remain unreedified, lyinge as desolate and voide groundes, and many of them adjoining nighe unto the highe streetes, replenished with muche odor, filthe and uncleanes, with the pytts, sellars, and vawtes lyinge open and uncovered, to the great perill and danger of all the inhabitants and other the king's subjects passing by the same; and some houses be verie weke and feeble, redy to fall down, and be verie dangerouse to passe by . . .

Houses fallen into decay had to be rebuilt within two years, and new houses put up on void ground where there had been houses before within 45 years. The other towns mentioned included Cardiff, Swansea, Shrewsbury, Liverpool and Wigan. Exalted company for little Presteigne, though it was not so much smaller than the other towns in those days. It is likely that much of the Tudor work left in the town dates from the period of that Act.

Camden's description of the town in 1585, quoted in the last chapter, seems to show that Presteigne put its houses in order after the Act and ceased to be " replenished with muche odor." Saxton in 1610 was even more convincing. He said:—

> Prestayn for beauteous building is the best in this Shire, a Towne of Commerce, wonderfully frequented, and that very lately.

The manufacture of woollen cloth was started in the town during Elizabeth's reign. This appears to have been carried on in buildings by the river. A writer in Archæologia Cambrensis, 1864, mentions that there were traces of buildings used for the purpose on both sides of the river. The business belonged to John Beddoes, who founded a Grammar School for boys at Presteigne in 1565, one of the very few in Wales at that date, and made other benefactions to the town. He placed the school in St. David's Street.

In the midst of all this prosperity, Presteigne came under grave affliction in the shape of a series of pestilences. Plagues were the terror of England before and after Elizabeth's reign. They were largely due to bad sanitation and lack of fresh air in the houses. The cumulative effect of continual burials within the churches, without the use of coffins, has also been held responsible. The first of which there is a record at Presteigne occurred in 1551, and was known as " the sweat." The countryfolk, with their grim sense of humour, called it " the new acquaintance "; they called the cholera when it first appeared " the new delight." This 1551 visitation, which generally killed those afflicted within seven or eight hours, began at Shrewsbury, and passed through Ludlow, Presteigne, and other places in South Wales on to Coventry, Oxford, and London.

The next plague epidemic occurred in 1593. We know something about this, because the church registers had been started then, and a *p* was put against the name of each person who had died from the plague. The average number of deaths each year about that time was 50, but in 1593 there were 383 deaths, of which the plague accounted for 352.*

There was another plague visitation in 1610, when the register recorded a total of 161 deaths, but did not mark those due to the plague. The next, and last recorded, plague was in 1636 and 1637, and, coming on top of the others, plunged the town into sore distress and poverty—so much so that the magistrates of the Hundred of Wigmore levied sums to be paid weekly by each parish in the Hundred in aid of the stricken town. There were 146 deaths from the plague in 1636 and 57 in 1637.

The country people did not dare to come near the town, and left their produce and the necessaries they brought for the relief of the inhabitants some distance out. One of the places they came to was the turning off the Combe road to Whitewall Farm, still known to some of the older inhabitants as Market Lane. Another was the grassy lane which runs from Brink Farm to Letchmoor Lane, and which preserved its traditional name of Chicken Lane until the last century.

---

* *See* Woolhope Transaction, 1859, for the figures quoted in this and the following sentences.

No more outbreaks of plague are recorded, but it might be mentioned here that there were bad smallpox epidemics in 1759, when the register records 22 deaths from this disease out of a total of 56, and in 1767, when the disease caused 27 deaths out of 48.

Presteigne has certainly been an unlucky place in the matter of " visitations," for there was another in 1682, in the shape of a fire. The town, in fact, seems to have copied London, in its plagues and " Great Fire." This fire must have been a very big one, and burnt down no small part of the town. In those days, and up to the early 19th century, " briefs " were issued by Royal Letters Patent when any town was in serious trouble, authorising collections in churches all over the land on behalf of the town. Many churches were built by this means. A brief was issued for Presteigne on account of the fire, through which the loss was put at £6,150,* a huge sum for that period.

It is rather striking that, in spite of the plague, Charles I required £28 for his ship money in 1636 from Presteigne, and only £6 from the Borough of New Radnor. It shows how far Presteigne had outstripped the old county town.

There was a curious transaction in 1634 which seems worth relating, as showing the state of the royal exchequer at that time. As has already been stated, the Mortimer possessions went to the Crown when Edward IV became king. They ultimately constituted what was known as the Lordship of Maelienydd, in which the manor of Presteigne was included.† Charles disposed of his rights to this lordship, but he had reckoned without the tenants and other inhabitants. They were proud of being directly under the Crown, and resented the new owners and their exactions, with the result that a public fund was opened and £741 12s. raised, a sufficient sum to re-purchase the lordship, and give it back to the king. Charles duly accepted the gift, resumed his position of overlord, and confirmed the ancient rights and privileges of the inhabitants.

---

* *See* Church Plate of Radnorshire (p. 40), by the Rev. J. T. Evans.

† The Lordship of Maelienydd appears to have included rather more than the original cantref of that name, since Presteigne, Radnor, and other places, now included in the Lordship, had previously, before the time of Henry VIII, formed separate lordships.

VII

Cavalier and Roundhead

Presteigne saw what was almost the first fighting of the Civil War. It happened in this way. The Parliament forces, under the Earl of Stamford, having seized Hereford, the Royalists of Herefordshire and Radnorshire set about raising a force to take the city. For this purpose their leaders met together at Presteigne. To this meeting, which happened in October, 1642, came Lord Herbert (son of the Marquis of Worcester), FitzWilliam Coningsby (M.P. for Herefordshire), and various other notables, including Charles Price of Pilleth, M.P. for Radnorshire. Unluckily for them, the Earl of Stamford came to know about the meeting, and sent some 60 horsemen, under a man named Fleming, who knew the neighbourhood, to arrest the leaders.

Fleming and his men arrived about 10 p.m., by which time Lord Herbert and most of the others had gone home. Those who remained were making merry at the house of Francis Rickards, Clerk of the Peace. The soldiers were probably doing the same elsewhere. At any rate, there was no proper guard, and Fleming had an easy job. There was a lot of noise, and firearms were discharged, with the result that three Welshmen fell and the rest fled; and Charles Price, Rickards, and some others were taken to Hereford at the tails of the horses of their captors.

Charles Price was released later, only to meet his death two years afterwards at Presteigne, where it is said he was stabbed by Colonel Robert Sandys. Price was a brave man, who stuck to his principles; he was known as the Prince of Radnorshire, where he had great influence. His widow, Margaret, was granted possession of Mynachty by order of Prince Rupert.*

At the beginning of the Civil War Radnorshire, like most of the rest of Wales, was Royalist in its sympathies. This was natural in a country where the old families had remained at home and had married with the yeoman class, where farm servants lived with their masters, and where the prosperous tradesmen of the towns had hardly penetrated, or revolutionary ideas gained a footing.

---

* Much of the information in this and the preceding paragraph is taken from Memorials of the Civil War in Herefordshire, by the Rev. John Webb.

For somewhat similar reasons, the rites and practices of the un-reformed Church had lingered longer in Wales than elsewhere (and may still be traced in some present-day customs). The king's armies were composed largely of Welshmen. Many entered or were pressed into his service from Presteigne and its neighbour-hood.

Among the few families with Puritan sympathies in the district were the Harleys of Brampton Bryan (forerunners of the Earls of Oxford). The siege of Brampton Bryan Castle and its brave and successful defence by Lady Brilliana Harley in 1643 are not especially connected with Presteigne, but they may be mentioned in passing, because the Royalist force, under Sir William Vavasour, sent to besiege the castle, came through Presteigne, from where Vavasour sent a letter to Prince Rupert of his intentions (in which he failed). There is extant a letter of Lady Brilliana, who wrote: " The prest soulders in Presteene have fought; and they say if it had not bine for the Trained Band they had killed the Captaine that is come down for them, refusing to goo with him because he is a Papis."

Another and a larger army passed through Presteigne. This was in August, 1645, after the battle of Naseby, when Charles was trying to avoid the Scottish army and making for Oxford. For-tunately for Presteigne, his army, some 4,000 strong, did not stay in the town, but went on towards Wigmore. This is what hap-pened near that place, according to a letter written at the time:

> There were one hundred quartered at Mr. Corkeram's house; and notwithstanding his complyancy both before and now, in the morning they killed some of his milch kine and all his sheep they could light of; and after they had drank out all the beer and ale that was in a poor man's house a dying, they plundered him of all his goods.

It seems worth while repeating this, because it shows the kind of thing people had to put up with as the war progressed. No wonder a Peace Army was formed in Wales, and farmers and others began to band together to protect their property from Cava-lier and Roundhead alike. One side was as bad as the other. About 500 men on the march over the hills near New Radnor, under Sir William Vaughan, descended on Trewern, and plundered it to the extent of £600. Some Parliament men pillaged Willey Court, some two miles from Presteigne, and molested the female servants, while the men were at work in the fields. When the owner found what had happened, he and his men, armed with pitchforks, chased the soldiers to Knighton, where they ran a fork into one and killed him, and maimed some of the others. A granddaughter of the above owner (Col. William Legge) married Joseph Beebee of Willey Hall, and thus became an ancestress of the Beebees of Womaston.

King Charles put up at the Bush, just outside Presteigne parish, when his army was on its way to Oxford. Sir Henry Slingsby, in his diary, tells how " the king lay in a poor, low chamber, and my Lord of Lindsay and others by the kitching fire, on hay "; and how, there being only one cheese for all, the good wife of the house " comes into the room where the king was, and very soberly asks if the king had done with the cheese, for the gentlemen without desired it." Tradition has it that when Charles found the place was named the Bush, he said it should be called the Beggar's Bush : and so the name remains.*

An interesting memento of the king's visit is preserved by the Rev. Claud Lewis at Evancoyd Court, near the Bush. This is a silver-handled rapier, which was found about a century ago in a pool in the Court grounds, and passed to its present owner from the Mynors family. Charles is said to have entered the grounds by a gate which was afterwards called the Royal Gate, and is now known as Railsgate. The story goes that he threw the rapier into the pool so that it might not betray him.

He was at Presteigne again in September, 1645, on his way from Hereford to Chester. The church register tells us that he spent two nights at Lower Heath, the house of Nicholas Taylor. Here his accommodation would be better, for Taylor, besides being a Royalist, was a wealthy man for these parts. From Lower Heath the king and his attendants appear to have ridden along Hoarstone Lane, and at what is still called the King's Turning turned right, in the direction of Stocking Farm and the road over the hills to Knighton, from where he is known to have reached Newtown the same night.

In connection with Nicholas Taylor, it will interest some readers to know that one of his grand-daughters married the son of Francis Rickards, mentioned at the beginning of this chapter, and that the Mynors family of Barland were directly descended from this marriage, a later Rickards changing his name to Mynors. John Rickards, the son in question, has a memorial tablet in Old Radnor Church.

In spite of the ebbing fortunes of the king, Presteigne remained faithful to his cause. Hope sprang up again with the outbreak of

---

* Perhaps the king had in mind the comedy of this name by Beaumont and Fletcher. Pepys referred to this play in his Diary, 3rd Jan., 1661 : " To the theatre, where was acted the Beggar's Bush, it being very well done, and here the first time that ever I saw women come upon the stage."

the second Civil War in 1648, and some Roundheads who were in the town were promptly put under lock and key. But it was acting for a lost cause. Hearts were still willing, and when Charles II came south three years later with his Scottish army, a small force of armed horsemen set out from Presteigne and joined the troop of the Duke of Buckingham at the fatal battle of Worcester. From a report of the Commissioners for Sequestration for South Wales we know the name of some of these Presteigne stalwarts—Nicholas Meredith, William Taylor, Thomas Gomey, John Bull, Andrew Higgins. They had to pay for their loyalty at the hands of the Commissioners, who had been appointed by Parliament to find out all who had at any time acted as Royalists and to sequester their estates or inflict heavy fines on them.

There were three of these Commissioners for each of the six South Wales counties. They worked under a body known as the Committee for Compounding, which sat in London. The correspondence between the Commissioners and the Committee has been preserved, and tells us much about Royalist " delinquents " in Radnorshire. One of the Commissioners' reports gives a vivid description of their difficulties. Here are two extracts:—

(1) The inferior people are so overawed by the malignant gentry that they make no conscience of wilful perjury, and publicly confess that they will not offend their landlords, come what may.

(2) We cannot improve what is under sequestration, nor discover who is liable thereto, as these six counties are very spacious, and the inhabitants, especially those that are guilty, are so rude and barbarous that nothing can be had from them but what is wrested by force.

The Commissioners did, in fact, get very little out of Radnorshire, which was never a county for tale-bearing where the law was concerned. One of them in disgust lampooned the county in these lines:

Radnorsheer, poor Radnorsheer,
Never a park and never a deer,
Never a squire of five hundred a year,
But Richard Fowler of Abbey Cwmhir.

Curiously, the Commissioners got far more out of Papists in Radnorshire than " delinquents," showing that the unreformed church was still strong in the county. One of their difficulties was getting the money they received to the Committee in London. They got over this in some instances by entrusting it to the Welsh cattle drovers, whose services were often thus made use of in their regular journeys to and from England, from Tudor times up to the coming of the railways.

Before leaving the subject of the Commissioners we will deal with the story of *John Bradshaw,* because it has been widely circulated that the regicide of this name was a native of Presteigne, or lived in the town. Apparently Williams, the county historian, is responsible for the story; he said that the regicide was one of the Commissioners at Presteigne and " fixed his residence " there.

All the biographies of the regicide agree that he was born at Stockport, Cheshire, in 1602, and not one of them mentions any connection with Presteigne. The same applies to his brother Henry (born in 1600), who lived and died in Cheshire. At the time the Commissioners were sitting at Presteigne, Bradshaw was Chief Justice of Chester, Attorney-General of Chester and North Wales, Chancellor of the Duchy of Lancaster, and a member of the Council of State. Moreover, he had been given the Deanery of Westminster for his residence (and died there). The men who acted as Commissioners were very much under the thumb of the London Committee. Such names as are known include several who served as officers on the Parliament side in the Civil War, but none of any person of the rank of a Judge, much less that of a member of the Council of State.

There was, however, a John Bradshaw at Presteigne in those days, and there is little doubt that Williams, seeing the name, jumped to his conclusion (as he does elsewhere in his History). The Bradshaws of Presteigne were, in fact, one of the leading families of the county. Lewis Dunn, in his book of pedigrees, written in 1597, said they came from Lancaster in 1540. A John Bradshaw witnessed a Presteigne will in 1544. Another John Bradshaw appeared in a list of Radnorshire gentry in 1602, included in George Owen's " Description of Wales."

The Rev. J. T. Evans says this man lived at the building now called the Radnorshire Arms. It will be noted that he was living at Presteigne the year in which the regicide was born at Stockport. The name is still found in the neighbourhood of Presteigne. There may have been some connection between the two families, but there is not the slightest reason otherwise to connect the regicide with Presteigne.

The religious changes following the victory of Parliament affected Presteigne like the rest of the country. The rector,* who had only just succeeded in transforming the living from a vicarage into a rectory, and incidentally making it the most valuable living in the county, was " removed," and his pulpit was occupied by the itinerant preachers appointed by the Westminster Synod for the " godly instruction " of the people.

---

* This was the Rev. John Scull, who died in poverty in 1652, and is buried in the chancel of the church at Presteigne.

Among these preachers was Walter Cradock, a well-known Puritan leader, who founded a little sect of his own. What the people of Presteigne made of him and his fellow-preachers we do not know, nor whether it was a relief or not to them to have another rector back under Charles II.* Some who were faithful churchmen would mind, no doubt—like Nicholas Taylor, of whom it is recorded in the church register that he had to take his children elsewhere to be baptised during this period, because " there was noe lawful minister setled in our parish." The new rector lost no time in getting his tithes restored, and his ministrations were probably milder than those of the ferocious schoolmaster type of preacher who had been using his pulpit.

By the end of the Commonwealth period the Dissenters had established a fairly strong footing in Radnorshire. A number who had been forced to leave the county before the Civil War returned when the war was over, when also Cromwell settled some of his ex-service men in the county. Presteigne acquired a group of Quakers, of whom Peter Price, J.P., was the best-known member, and a personal friend of George Fox.

Many of the Radnorshire gentry remained faithful to the Stuart cause after the fall of James II. There is a tradition that Jacobite sympathisers planted Scotch pine trees by their houses as a token of their loyalty. The old man who related this tradition had frequently heard the trees called " Charlie trees," and this name persists to-day in some parts of the county. Until the last year (when the trees were cut down), there were some Scotch pines at Whitton Court, $3\frac{1}{2}$ miles from Presteigne, to which this story attached.

---

* We will hope that an entry in the church register of New Radnor against the death of a rector of rather later times is unique; this reads: " To the great joy of the inhabitants."

VIII

Forward

With the Civil War at an end and Charles II on the throne, Presteigne settled down into peaceable ways, and rapidly became a town of some respectability and importance, and the largest in the county. There appears to be no record of the date when it was first recognised officially as the county town instead of New Radnor. The latter place never wholly recovered after its destruction by the forces of Owen Glendower in 1401. But its castle stood until the Civil War (when it was destroyed by the Parliamentarians), and there is evidence that it provided the county with a gaol in some part of the 16th century. Perhaps the administration of the county was also carried out from the castle. The Minutes of the General Sessions at Presteigne start in 1753, and it is clear that the county gaol was then at Presteigne, and that both the legal and civil administration of the county (excepting the Borough of New Rednor) were looked after at Presteigne.

As we have already seen, the Great Sessions have usually been held at Presteigne since 1542. Here also came special Courts of Inquiry. At the Record Office, for instance, there is an account of an Inquisition taken at Presteigne in 1601 on the attainder of Sir Gelli Meyrick of Gladestry, after the latter had been hanged at Tyburn for his share in the rebellion of the Earl of Essex.* The latter, by the way, was a Herefordshire man, and lay rector of Presteigne.

At the time of the Rebecca Riots in 1843, when many toll gates up and down South Wales were destroyed by parties of disguised men,† the Government appointed a Royal Commission to inquire into the cause of the disturbances. This also came to Presteigne to hold its sittings. The Commissioners discovered some real grievances behind the disturbances, and brought about their removal. Some of the rioters, nevertheless, got 20 years' transportation.

---

* An interesting valuation is given of all the furniture, livestock, etc., of Sir Gelli, including the following: 10 oxen, £16; 14 kyns, £9 7s. 8d.; 4 steers, £4; 70 sheep, £8 10s.
† The men were usually disguised as women. Their original leader, Thomas Rees, was a man of great bulk, and is said to have borrowed his disguise from a woman of equal bulk known as " Great Rebecca of Llangolman," hence the nickname for the rioters.

Presteigne was also the headquarters of the Royal Radnor Militia, and here for over 200 years it was inspected and carried out its training, when not embodied for duty elsewhere. The earliest inspection of which there is a record was that made by the Duke of Beaufort, who, as Lord President of Wales, came to Presteigne in 1684 and saw the Militia, consisting of a troop of horse and three companies of foot, with yellow colours flying. We are told that " a good volley was given, and his Grace rode through the ranks of each company."

It is curious to read in a marching order of 1812 that the men were to have " their hair neatly tied behind and their Fals Queus and hair leather in their knapsacks." The Radnor Militia was united with the Brecon Militia in 1877, and in 1881 the new regiment was formed into the 3rd Battalion, the South Wales Borderers.* Mr. Charles Norman, who died at Presteigne in March, 1944 (aged 92), is believed to have been the last survivor of the Radnor Militia.

One or two writers seem to suppose that Presteigne was a larger place before its plague visitations than ever afterwards. There is no evidence to support this view. With one exception, the names of streets, etc., which occur in 16th century documents are the same as those we know to-day; a will of 1544 mentions Hereford Street and High Street, and another, of 1559, Broad Street, High Street, and Green End.

The exception is Ave Maria Lane, which cannot now be identified; it may have been the old name of St. David's Street and changed to that after the Reformation. (The name would be a good substitute for Back Lane or Chapel Terrace, two not very attractive names which now exist). Ford Street, across the Lugg, was known as Frog Street in former days. The writer has not found any early references to Scottleton Street. In several indentures of the period 1785-1810 the name is given as Scotland, and this was used by some people up to the 1890's. Scottleton may thus be a modern corruption, interesting as it sounds.

Presteigne remained the most important town in the county in the 18th century, and probably shared in the increased number of houses built in the county, as shown by D. J. Davies in his " Economic History of South Wales prior to 1800,"—according to which the number of houses in Radnorshire was 2,092 in 1708, 2,425 in 1750, 3,076 in 1781, and 3,675 in 1801.

---

* A very full and valuable account of the Militia in Radnorshire is given in Notes on the Militia, by Lt.-Col. G. Drage, published by the Radnorshire Society.

The town never shared the ancient distinction of New Radnor in being an incorporated borough. It claimed to be a borough by prescription, and the local guide books say it was, but the Municipal Corporations Commission of 1835 reported that there was "no trace of any charter or corporate office or jurisdiction."

Under the legislation of Henry VIII the elected burgesses of New Radnor, with those of Knighton, Rhayader, Knucklas, and Cefnllys, had the right of electing a Member of Parliament, who sat for what was known as the Radnor Boroughs. Another Member was elected by the rest of the county. Presteigne was included with the rest of the county, until the Reform Act of 1832 included it with the Radnor Boroughs. The county lost its privilege of returning two Members in 1884, and now returns one jointly with the county of Brecon.

The town formed a part of the manor of Presteigne, which, we have seen, was for centuries a royal manor (except during the Commonwealth, and for that short period when Charles I sold it, to have it returned to him by the inhabitants). Government was in the hands of a bailiff, under the chief steward of the manor, or his deputy. In earlier years the bailiff was termed the portreeve. A grant of 1485 (preserved at the British Museum) bestowed this office on Morys ap Rees.

Manorial courts were held regularly, at which a bailiff was elected each year, petty constables appointed, leases exchanged, withdrawn, or renewed, offenders against what we might term the local by-laws cited and punished, and the privileges of the community in general asserted and maintained. The court might inflict fines of any amount under £2, and distrain, if necessary, to recover the fine. This form of government still obtained when Williams wrote his history (about 1818). It is not known how long the Presteigne court continued to meet, but some other manorial courts in Radnorshire were held as late as 1864, and such courts were not abolished until the County Court Act of 1867 was passed.

The National Library at Aberystwyth has a document relating to the court held for the manor of Presteigne on 24th May, 1688.* This gives a good idea of the customs of the manor and rights and privileges claimed by the tenants. The bailiff " for all the tyme whereof the memory of man is not to the contrary, saveing only in the late time of rebellion," had a right to all the toll of corn and grain brought into and sold in the markets and fairs of the town, and " alsoe all the proffittes or rentes paid for standinges under the Sheirhall upon markette and faire days." In return he was expected to keep all the streets of the town in repair, and to spend at least £3 each year on such repairs.

---

* Printed in the Transactions of the Radnorshire Society, Vol. IV.

The tenants, the document proceeds, claimed " the benefitt and comodity of all their commons and wast lands within the precincts of the manor, and all their privilidges of buildinge penthouses upp into their ancient messuages in the said towne of Presteigne next the streets thereof for standings and sale of comodities on markettes and faire days there."

One of the offences most frequently brought before the manor courts was encroachment of the common and waste lands. Greedy tenants were constantly " trying it on " by putting up gates, hedges and fences, to add this or that piece of waste to their lawful holding. They were very soon reported and brought to book. It was left to the landlords of the 19th century, with their wholesale Enclosure Acts, to show the lawfulness and entire respectability of enclosures. A word about this later.

There was a case of the kind before this Presteigne court. On the information of John Burrnupp, constable of Hereford Street Ward, Stephen Willett was " presented " for putting up a gate at the head of a common lane which led to the wheat lands, " being a lane which alwayes lay open "; he was fined 10s. " if he doth not pluck the said gate or yeate cleerly away within the space of one moneth."

Here are some other fines of rather later date (1713-17) which were laid down at a neighbouring manor court, showing other types of offences which came before the courts. They certainly made for careful conduct on the part of the inhabitants:

> 6s. 8d. on a man for keeping his cattle about the lanes and destroying his neighbour's hedges.
> 6s. 8d. for allowing swine to go unringed.
> 2s. 6d. on some women for " Sabbath breaking and tale bearing."
> 3s. 4d. on all parents and children " going to prophane the Lord's Day."
> 6s. 8d. on certain persons for selling ale and receiving people's servants on Saturday nights and Sabbath days.
> 13s. 4d. for keeping an inmate and her child.*
> 6s. 8d. for not scouring a low ditch.

Some of the following Elizabethan by-laws might not be popular to-day. The last was made at a time when foreign invasion threatened England:

> Everyone to go to church or pay 1s. fine for each offence.

---

* Every parish was watchful about strangers, for fear they might become chargeable to the parish poor fund.

Every inhabitant within the borough shall warn their children that they must not play in the churchyard and break the glass windows, in pain for every default 4d.

No person or persons within the borough shall scolde or chide the one upon the other but that they show their default to the bailiff and the bailiff to redress the default in pain of 3s. 4d.

All men servants and all inhabitants shall not haunt the ale houses or streets without a lawful cause after 7 p.m. in the winter and 8 p.m. in summer, in pain of punishment by the officers.

Everyone above the age of 12 years and is able to shoot shall follow their bows and apply themselves to " arty-lerrye," and that they do not play at ball or any unlawful games.

The Sessional Rolls show that in 1792 the magistrates appointed the petty constables for the town, because the manor court had not met that year.

The cloth manufacturing industry established by John Beddoes in the reign of Queen Elizabeth was " irreparably damaged " by the pestilence of 1636-37, according to Williams. A small woollen factory was started in the town soon after 1755, under the encouragement of the Breconshire Agricultural Society. This flourished for a time and received Army contracts, but had ceased to exist by 1840. It occupied the three-storeyed buildings by the river, now known as Riverside Villas.

There were also several fulling mills in the town and neighbourhood, which helped farmers to produce woollen goods from their own wool. Carding, spinning, and knitting were staple home industries in those days, especially the knitting of long woollen stockings, worn by men and women alike, the wool (from black sheep) being spun at home, as was also flax (for sheets, etc.) on many of the outlying farms.

It was on its corn trade, however, that Presteigne chiefly relied for its prosperity in the 18th century—that and its malthouses and inns. Kitchin, in his map of Radnorshire of about 1750, says of Presteigne: " It is a large, well-built and populous town, where the Assizes are held and the county gaol kept. The market is much resorted to and well furnished with provisions and grain, especially barley. Its chief trade is in malt." Brookes, in his General Gazeteer of 1766, describes the town as handsome, with paved regular streets, and says the market " is remarkable for barley, of which they make a great deal of malt."

To show the importance of its corn market in those days, it should be added that the town had an official with the duty of making weekly returns of the prices realised for corn. The Sessional Rolls show payments for such returns up to 1813.

The market day was Saturday until 1841, when it was changed to Tuesday. It was later changed to Wednesday, and this has been the market day for at least 60 years. But how different were the markets of that time ago from those of the present! In those days there were no auctions. Sales were effected between seller and buyer direct. The animals filled the streets, pens being provided for sheep and pigs. Bargains were usually concluded at an inn, not infrequently inducing that state of merriment for the journey home known in Radnorshire as " market peart."

Many of the cottage women from the surrounding country walked four or five miles to attend the market, with a heavy basket slung over each arm, often knitting every yard of the journey, making the black stockings spoken of above. A farmer, long since dead, used to tell how he once gave one of these a lift, and, noticing that she was nursing her heavy baskets, asked why she did not put them on the floor of the gig. The gentle old soul replied that she was trying to ease the horse's burden. We may smile at her simplicity. Yet that thoughtfulness for another has its touching side, in one accustomed to burdens probably all her life.

For a short time an attempt was made to grow flax in the county on a considerable scale, in addition to the usual corn crops. Under an Act of 1786 the Government paid a bounty of 4d. per stone on the flax raised, but the effort does not appear to have been successful, and the Rolls show no claimants after 1796. There were two claimants at Presteigne and one at Whitton, but only for a year or two. Some farmers, however, grew small quantities of flax up to the 1830's or 1840's, in order to meet the requirements of the home spinning wheel. Rye was grown on the higher lands up to the late 1870's, and a mixture of wheat and rye flour was often used for the home-made bread. It is interesting to note that Radnorshire farmers have started to grow rye again during the present war, though not in the Presteigne area.

IX

Backward

The Rev. J. T. Evans, in his Church Plate of Radnorshire, judging from the number of " houseling " people (i.e., those 14 years of age and over) given for 1548, estimated that the population of Presteigne at that date was about 750. The Census figures for the civil parish are as follows:

1801	...	1,057	1871	... 1,713
1811	...	1,114	1881	... 1,491
1821	...	1,288	1891	... 1,360
1831	...	1,513	1901	... 1,245
1841	...	1,407	1911	... 1,141
1851	...	1,453	1921	... 1,172
1861	...	1,603	1931	... 1,102

The plagues of 1551 and 1593 probably carried off at least half the population. There were over 100 deaths from plague in 1610, and 200 in 1636-37. Yet it remained the county Assize town, was a centre of some importance in the Civil War, and retained its corn market. We can only assume that newcomers soon filled up the gaps. They would come from the English side of the border, rather than the sparsely populated Welsh side. Perhaps that explains why such a high percentage of the population have English names, Welsh names being in a decided minority.

The population of the whole county of Radnor was 19,050 in 1801, and had increased to only 21,323 in 1931. This is equivalent to 45 persons to the square mile, no other county in England or Wales having such a small density. Llandrindod Wells in 1801 was only a village; in 1931 it had a population of 2,925, an increase which more than swallows up the county increase—which might otherwise have been an actual decrease.

The figures for Presteigne show that the population in 1931 was much about what it was 130 years previously, and that since 1871, when it reached its highest point, there has been a reduction of over one-third.

When Williams wrote his history, the town had lost much of its trade to Knighton and Kington. This was probably due in large measure to the new turnpike roads, which were constructed after 1780. As was mentioned on page 22, Presteigne in ancient times lay across some important roads. These lost much of their importance when the new roads were opened, especially the one from Aberystwyth into England through New Radnor and Kington. Both Knighton and Kington are better centres than Presteigne, and it is easy to understand how they came to outstrip Presteigne.

Presteigne had begun to strike hard times before the end of the 18th century. The Revolutionary and French wars resulted in high prices, which benefited the farmers, but not the wage-earners, who got only small increases in their wages. In 1795 farm workers received 1s. a day in the winter and 1s. 6d. in the summer, with beer in addition; women's wages were 6d. a day, also with beer. At the woollen factory men got 9s. a week, women 4s. 6d. to 5s., and children 1s. 6d.; women knitting for hire at home got 6d. a day. Wages were so small in proportion to prices that it was said the poor were literally starving.* There were at that time about 230 houses in the town, and no less than 65 families were in receipt of outdoor relief, while the workhouse had 19 inmates.

Matters became worse at the end of the French war, when prices rose far beyond wages. The Sessional Rolls show that while bread was sold at 4d. per 4½ lb. in 1817, in 1820 the price was 9d. for 4 lb. Farmers began to lay down their arable land to grass, and the poor rate rose by one-half its former figure. Many families were compelled to leave the land for the towns, and by 1836 wages had been lowered to 6s. a week.† The decline in the rural population is reflected in the County Census figures for 1851, which showed a decline for the first time since 1801.

How far the general depression affected Presteigne it is diffi-cult to say, but it seems possible that the increase in its population in 1831 was due in some part to people coming into the town who could not find employment on the farms. The rapid extension of the iron and coal industries drew away many people from the county into the new industrial centres after 1840. This movement of the population unfortunately continued until at least the 1890's. There can be few counties with so many derelict or pulled-down little homesteads scattered up and down the countryside as Rad-norshire.

There was another cause for this rural decay which should be mentioned. The enclosure of the common and waste lands in Rad-norshire did not start in real earnest until 1810. From that year to 1868 there were 30 Enclosure Acts; these, with four more from 1868 to 1882, enclosed a total of at least 45,000 acres. At the end

---

* *See* the Economic History of South Wales prior to 1800, by D. J. Davies.

† *See* the Economic History of South Wales, by Evan J. Jones.

BROAD STREET   *Shire Hall on right.*

BROAD STREET   *Well House in foreground, Old Oak Inn next door.*

(To face page 48*).*

HIGH STREET   *Assembly Rooms at end.*

HIGH STREET—*Castle Inn in fore-*
ground, old Posting House (New Inn)
at end.

SCOTTLETON STREET   *Old Bell Inn in foreground.*

(To face page 49).

of the 18th century 200,000 acres (or two-thirds of the county) are said to have been unenclosed.*

Williams said that two-thirds of the parish of Presteigne were unenclosed. There was no Act which would account for the enclosure of the latter, nor for that matter of a great part of the rest of the unenclosed land in the county. We can only conclude it was done by other means.† In any case, the Acts were easily obtained by the gentry who wanted the land, and there was little chance of successful resistance by those directly affected, since there was no appeal beyond the Quarter Sessions, where the Bench was composed of the very people who got the land, or their friends.

Enclosures were not necessarily a bad thing, though they led to the eviction of many crofters or smallholders, and it is to be feared some individuals were more concerned with the sporting rights they acquired thus cheaply, rather than with " the cultivation and improvement " of the land, which the Acts said was the reason for handing it over to them. The woodlands had previously been neglected, but now were turned to some account, to the benefit of the new owners and the community alike. Improved methods of cultivating the land were also introduced.

All this led to an increase of employment at first. Later, with the consolidation of holdings, fewer labourers were needed, and the small farmers also suffered, so that in the end enclosures undoubtedly contributed to rural depopulation, as well as to the substitution of a dependent wage-earning class for an independent class of smallholder.

It is to be feared this chapter reads too much like a treatise on economics. But it has been trying to show some of the causes for the curious change in the population figures up to 1851—the flight from country to town, combined with the flight from both country and small town—a flight which was unfortunately resumed after 1871 and has continued ever since ‡

Dugdale wrote in 1843 that the town was the handsomest and best built in the county, but there was little trade. Malting continued to be the principal industry at this period. In Lewis's Topographical Dictionary of 1845 we read that the principal trade was malt, " the soil being favourable to barley," and that there

---

* See the Economic History of South Wales prior to 1800, by D. J. Davies.

† Probably for the most part by purchase from the Commissioners of Woods and Forests, who sold most of the Crown property comprised in the wastes and commons of the county.

‡ There was an appreciable amount of emigration to Canada and Australia from Presteigne about the period 1910-12.

was some trade in timber and coal. Lewis also said that the streets were partially paved, but not lighted, and that water was supplied, by means of pump and wells.

Some new businesses appear to have been started in the town between 1851 and 1871, and conditions improved for a time. The principal businesses at this period, besides the malt houses, were the spittle-tree (spade-handle) factory of John Weaver, the tannery and saw-mill of Thomas Lewis, and Davies's cooperage.

Weaver's factory was situated by the Barley Mow in Hereford Street, and he built for his workmen the brick houses near that inn and those in Gas House Row opposite. This business employed from 30 to 40 workpeople. It gradually fell off under foreign competition, and was closed in the 1880's, after John Weaver's death in 1882. The tannery and saw-mill business, situated by the river, where a laundry is now carried on, went on rather longer, John Price taking it over when Thomas Lewis died. The cooperage was up Green End.

The town had a straw hat factory in 1840, but nothing is now known as to its whereabouts or subsequent career. A rope-walk, which was situated near the tannery, has also passed out of living memory. A Ludlow firm had a flourishing brick-making business near Radnor Wood Farm (now a ruin), which came to an end in the early 1890's. Traces of the workings may still be seen. (Bricks were also made at Combe Moor in the 18th century.)

Presteigne still had several malthouses in the 1850's, notably one where is now Hill's factory (once the electricity supply station) at the bottom of Harper Street, one in the building now occupied by the Capital Stores in High Street, one on the present site of the Midland Bank in Hereford Street, and one belonging to John Weaver at the Barley Mow. These mostly ceased to exist in the 1880's,* though " Jones the Maltster " continued his business on the factory site until about 1892. There was also a nail factory belonging to Edward Newell behind the shop still occupied by that family in Broad Street; this was closed in 1888.

In the 1840's and 1850's Presteigne, in addition to the above businesses, had its own patten makers, boot makers, pump makers, clock makers, etc. Most small towns were self-supporting in those days, and indeed until the railways came, to bring the products of the large towns and drive the small man out of business.

---

* The Free Mash Tun Act of 1880, by abolishing the malt tax and putting the duty on the extract or wort from the malt, favoured the large breweries and largely put the small man out of business, since he could not extract his malt as economically as the former.

Nor should we forget the Lancashire clog makers, who regularly visited the district each summer for many years, and indeed only ceased to come about 40 years ago. They usually came in a party of about a dozen, living in tents by the river. They cut down the alder trees themselves, and shaped clogs on the spot.

Unsuccessful efforts were made in the early 19th century to get coal at Presteigne, on the south side near the Clatter Brook. Borings were again made round the year 1912, but met with similar failure; tracings of the workings may still be seen on the hillside beyond the County School. The Woolhope Transactions of 1912 said that fragments of coal were occasionally picked up on Cole's Hill.

With nothing to take the place of the above manufacturing businesses, it is not surprising that Edwin Davies wrote in his 1905 edition of Williams's History that " the town does not now present an appearance of much business activity." In fact, it had, from that point of view, become once more the " decayed " town of the Act of 1544.

It is still the Assize town of the county, and in name at least is the county town. The Standing Joint Committee (the Police Authority for the county) held its meetings at the Shire Hall until June, 1899, but the administrative work of the county has been carried on from Llandrindod Wells since 1889. The County Court was transferred to Knighton in 1941.

There was for many years a Presteigne Penny Bank, but this was closed in 1893. At present there are two Banks, Lloyds and the Midland, Barclays Bank having closed its Presteigne branch in 1942. There are monthly cattle auctions, which are held on the first Wednesday.

Before concluding this chapter, something should be said about the corn mills of the neighbourhood, once so important a feature of every town and manor. Here came the grain, threshed by hand,* the larger quantities piled on farm wagons, the smaller slung in bags on the back of a horse or donkey, to be taken home again in the form of flour or meal. Here, too, came the gleaners carrying their small gains. It was a recognised custom after harvest for them to be admitted to the fields and treated to a hearty meal by the farmer whose land they " leased." "A gooding, a gooding, to make me a pudding," was the rhyme repeated by the cottagers when later, on St. Thomas's Day, they visited each farm in turn, asking for gifts of flour.

---

* The flail is still used on some of the small holdings around Radnor Forest.

The Water Company's pumping station is now housed in the building of the Presteigne mill, situated on the south bank of the river, by the path leading to Boultibrooke. This, known as the New Mill, was worked as a corn mill until 1908. The present building appears to be 17th century, though there was probably a mill on the same site from at least the 15th century. Stapleton had a mill in the 14th century, and still has a building of that period (Carter's Croft), which may have been that mill.

St. Mary Mill (pronounced locally as Semery, sometimes Sembley), rather more than a mile along the road to Discoed, is reputed to have belonged in medieval times to the Nunnery of Limebrook, which held lands at Presteigne. According to a Norton Manor roll of 1694, the mill itself was on the Lugg, opposite the present building which bears its name. There is an ancient mill at Norton, and this is still working. Boultibrooke Mill is mentioned in the same document of 1694. It was working 100 years later, but appears to have been closed in the early 19th century, to be used as the home laundry. The building may still be seen in the Boultibrooke grounds.

On the other side of Presteigne, Wegnall Mill was only closed about 1934; the building is of the 17th century. According to documents of the 16th century, there was a mill on the Lugg near Broad Heath—probably at Letchmoor Farm, from which a water wheel was removed in the 1920's—but nothing is known of its history.

It is sad to think that so many mills are no more, and that no longer do people bake their own bread from local stone-ground flour. If meat was a rare item on the labourer's table 60 or 80 years ago, such foods as home-made bread, butter, and cheese, and the homely buttermilk, with the oaten concoction known as flummery (once a universal dish in Radnorshire), probably more than made up for the deficiency. The discontinuance of the old mills may well be noted in a chapter entitled " Backward."

X

Yesterday and To-day

Employment in the town remained at the low ebb noted in 1905 by Edwin Davies up to practically the outbreak of the present war. At any rate, little had arisen to take the place of the old industries. The main sources of employment continued to be agriculture and estate work, and the limestone quarries at Nash. Within the last few years a small factory has been started for the manufacture of light die castings, which has added appreciably to the volume of employment, particularly for women and girls. Another new venture has been the cultivation of medicinal herbs on a large scale, which, with bulb growing (practised in the neighbourhood for some years), promises to become of some importance. Thus at the present time the outlook as regards employment appears brighter than for some years.

On the whole, it would seem that after it lost its corn market Presteigne prospered most about the period 1855-1885. It was during this period that the Assembly Rooms, with the market hall below,* at the corner of Broad Street and Hereford Street, were built (1865), and the railway extended to Presteigne (1874); likewise the " British " School in Hereford Street, which was opened in 1868, and transferred to the Radnorshire Education Authority in 1906, and the National (now C. of E.) School in Scottleton Street, which was opened in 1869.† Before these schools were opened, many of the Presteigne children had to walk to the Whitton school, a distance of four miles. Children of six did this journey of eight miles there and back.

Three of the Free Churches held services in the town in the early part of the 19th century, but the Baptists did not have a church of their own until 1845; this (in Hereford Street) was renovated and improved in 1875, and enlarged in 1885. The Wesleyan church in St. David's Street, now closed, was opened in 1870, and the Primitive Methodist (now Methodist) church, opposite Warden

---

* The market hall is now (1945) used as a fire station. The name Assembly Rooms appears to have arisen only with the present building. It was used in the 1870's.

† These schools are known in the town as the *bottom* and *top* schools, respectively—terms of location only.

Lane, in 1867; the Primitive Methodists previously worshipped in the building known as Old Chapel in Harper Street, which was built in the 1830's.

None of the above buildings can be said to be much of an ornament to the town. Their smallness may be said to be their chief virtue, on the principle that the less such buildings hit the eye, the less we need think about them. From this point of view, the Assembly Rooms and the Methodist Church come off worst, and perhaps the railway station best.

Yet they are all buildings with a character of their own, and as such entitled to some respect, if not admiration. The same can hardly be said of the sham-Tudor building (Radnor Buildings), at the corner of Hereford Street and Green End, or of the monstrous group of three tall tenements at the corner of Chapel Terrace and High Street. The electricity supply standards are another un-decorative feature of the town, which it is to be hoped may be re-moved some day.

A word or two might be said here about the Baptists and other Free Church bodies. A return filed among the Shire Hall records shows that in 1830 there were in the town nine Baptists, sixteen Wesleyan Methodists and sixteen " Ranters " (Primitive Metho-dists); this is very different from the flourishing communities which exist to-day. The first Baptist minister was the Rev. D. Evans, who died in 1828. Services were at first held at a house in High Street, and later in an upper room behind Mr. Newell's shop in Broad Street. Baptisms took place in the river. The Primitive Methodists used to hold an open-air rally, which was attended by hundreds of people, on the Warden the Sunday before the Warden Wake. The day was known as Camp Meeting Sunday; it is still observed, though the procession which preceded it has been lacking since about 1928, and it is far from being the occasion of former years.

The Beddoes Grammar School, founded in 1565 (*see page* 33), had ups and downs of fortune. At one time it provided scholar-ships to Oxford, but in 1847 a Welsh Education Commissioner reported that the school was " grossly inefficient, the boys ignorant, the master incompetent, the trustees negligent, the building almost without furniture." A Commissioner of 1866 said that, in spite of a new building, it was " somewhat yet not greatly better." The " new building " referred to is the unattractive brick building on the north side of the churchyard. Matters improved later, and the school spread into Garrison House next door (after it had been vacated by the Militia in 1877), and to the house known as The Vyne, in St. David's Street (which was used for boarders). The school was closed in 1898, when its endowment fund passed to the

County Council and the pupils were transferred to the new County Secondary School.

The latter was formally opened by the Duke of Devonshire, 15th April, 1899, but teaching started there the previous October. Only boys were admitted at first; within two or three years girls were also admitted, and it has been a mixed school ever since. It occupies the site of the County Gaol, which was moved there from Broad Street in 1822, and incorporates much of the stonework of the gaol.

The British and National Schools have already been mentioned. Another school of some importance was Greenfields. This occupied the building on the west side of the churchyard, now used as the Church Hall. It was a girls' school, built and endowed in 1850 by Mrs. Evans in memory of her husband, the Rev. Samuel Evans. It had a useful existence until 1929, when the pupils were transferred to the National School. There was also a school for infants, established and maintained by Lady Brydges, of Boultibrooke. This was started after Greenfields, and closed in 1892. It was known locally as the Iron School, more vulgarly the Ragged School; its site, now covered with trees, may still be seen on the right-hand side of the path leading from West Wall to the pumping station.*

There were two private schools for girls which had a good reputation in their day. The earlier of these was kept by a Miss Blackburn, at Harford House, in Hereford Street. This was going in the 1860's and 1870's. The other, which ran into the 1880's, was kept by a Miss Newark at Ossington House (6, Broad Street).

The gas works, near the Clatter Brook end of Hereford Street, were opened with great ceremony in 1857. The coming of gas caused something of a sensation in the town. The magistrates at the Shire Hall hesitated for some time before adopting such an innovation. They submitted in 1860, but at first only to the extent of trying it in the kitchen and servants' hall. Trying it on the dog first, so to speak ! Kington had been lit by gas since 1830.

The telegraph came to Presteigne in 1870, but the town had to wait until 1920 for electric light. The original electricity supply station (at the bottom of Harper Street) belonged to a local company. The current is now brought to Presteigne by the Shropshire, Worcestershire and Staffordshire Electric Power Co. Previous to 1904 the town relied on its wells and pumps for its water

---

* The iron building was moved to the grounds of Boutibrooke, where it stands to-day.

supply; this is now in the hands of the Presteigne Water Company, and water is laid on to nearly every house. The pumping station occupies the building of the old corn mill (*see page* 52).

The town is under the local administration of an Urban District Council, which was formed under the Local Government Act, 1892. The area administered is 2,994 acres. The offices are at 43, High Street (Clerk, Cecil Sellers). This is merely a small shop converted for the purpose; doubtless after the present war more worthy quarters will be erected. The meetings of the Council are held at the Shire Hall.

The bungalow on the hill beyond the Warden, once known as the Harley Poultry Farm, was originally the town's isolation hospital. Many years ago the town had a " workhouse." This was described in 1790 as a " most wretched hovel." No one now knows where it was; it was probably closed after the Poor Law Amendment Act of 1834 was passed. Within recent years out-of-works on the tramp (" travellers," as they are called in Radnorshire) found cheap lodgings (4d. a night) at the old house, 16, Hereford Street.

At the Slough (pronounced Slew) there has been during the present war an important depot for the Radnorshire War Agricultural Executive Committee. The same site previously served for a Training Centre of the Ministry of Labour.

A curious feature of Presteigne is that, although many of its buildings are named for postal and registration purposes, there is hardly a house or shop which shows its name. It is a pity, because much may be learnt from some of the names—those, for instance, which embody the names of old inns or indicate a past use long forgotten.

Garrison House, on the north-west side of the churchyard, was the depot of the Royal Radnor Militia from 1855 to 1877. The Old Rectory, near the church in Broad Street, was used as the rectory until 1849, when the present large house in St. David's Street, previously known as Great House, took its place. The building known as the Police Station, near Hill's factory in Harper Street, and now used as a telephone exchange, ceased to be a police station in 1932, since when the sergeant has been housed in the Shire Hall, and his assistant at the separate station at 8, Hereford Street. The house called The Temple, near the County School, is reputed to have been occupied in the mid-nineteenth century by a certain disreputable character, who was generally known as Sodom, and whose house came to be known as Sodom's Temple; the latter part of the name has persisted.

The parish church and inns of the town are dealt with in separate chapters. The town stocks were placed at the Bull Hotel corner of St. David's Street. This corner, until about 60 years ago, was known as Skin Cross Corner. A petrol pump now stands on the site of the stocks, and a garage has replaced the old cottages which, within living memory, overlooked the spot. Opposite, in the garden of the Radnorshire Arms, was a great larch tree (cut down these 20 years past), under whose spreading branches the town loafers for generations used to collect. The last recorded case in this country of a person being put in the stocks was at Newbury in 1872. The Presteigne stocks were removed shortly before that date.

Many of the older inhabitants remember a stout wooden post which stood at Skin Cross Corner. An old man, long since dead, said he had heard this post was used for bull-baiting. Hence perhaps the name given to the hotel nearby. It is known that this cruel sport (with dogs) was practised at Kington as late as 1815.

Fastened to an ancient sycamore in Norton churchyard are two pairs of very old handcuffs. They are quite unusual, and may have been used for a pillory. We do not know where the Presteigne pillory was, but very likely it was near the position of the stocks. Every market town had one from the time of Henry III. The walls of the pound (or pinfold), used for stray animals until modern times, may be seen at the small road-fork at the bottom of Chapel Terrace. The Market Hall stood on the site of the present Assembly Rooms. There was a public room above, which was probably used as the Town Hall (referred to several times in the old Sessional Minutes), as it certainly was for concerts and other public functions.

Another corner of which the old name is almost forgotten is at the Kington turning by Greenfields house. This was formerly known as Dick Green's Corner, after a highwayman of that name who was buried there, after his execution at Gallows Lane. His ghost was long believed to haunt the spot, which was the scene of his last exploit—in spite of the fact that a stake had been driven through his heart.

There remains to be mentioned the Shire Hall, the most important building of all, since it gives the town its title to be the county town. The present building in Broad Street was opened in 1830. Its style is much what we should expect of that period, and might have been worse. It has a notable collection of oil paintings of prominent men of the county, and contains furnished quarters for the accommodation of the visiting judges.

Various kinds of public functions used to take place at the Shire Hall. Presteigne had to wait until 1882 for its Blue Ribbon Army, but there was a Temperance Lecture at the Hall in 1860—probably the first of its kind to be heard at Presteigne. It was a custom, continued into modern times, for each new magistrate, on his appointment to the General Sessions, to make a contribution to the wine cellar of the Shire Hall, which enjoyed a well-deserved reputation. It is to be presumed that the lecturer on this occasion was not asked to dine with the magistrates. The Militia band concerts were given at the Hall in the 1860's, and here in 1874 was held a grand fancy dress ball, to celebrate the opening of the railway to Presteigne.

The Shire Hall before 1830 stood at the corner of Broad Street and High Street, and the old county gaol occupied the present site of the Shire Hall. The latter, as already stated, was moved to the site now occupied by the County School, near the Clatter Brook. There is a drawing made in 1832 by the local artist, J. M. Ince, which shows both the new Shire Hall and the old one. This appears to have been a two-storied building of the 17th or early 18th century, the hall and other apartments above supported by pillars, which stretched across a part of the street as we know it to-day. There was thus an arcade below the hall, which was used by stallholders on market days. The post office and the house attached now stand on the old site. Some of the cellarage of the old building remains, in particular a room known as the Ivory Chamber.

Ince's picture shows Broad Street as cobbled. Presteigne preserved a good deal of its pitching up to about 40 years ago, and pieces of cobbled pavement and carriage ways are still to be seen in front of or behind some of the houses in every street.

Another relic of old times which is happily still preserved is the " zig-zag " bridge over the Lugg. This probably dates back to the 16th century at least.

The site of the castle, destroyed in 1262, may be plainly seen on the Warden, the mound of the keep (reduced from its original height by constant removal of the earth*) appearing within the earthen foundations of the courtyard walls. The Warden was presented to the town in 1805 by the fifth Earl of Oxford, whose brother was rector of Presteigne up to the time of his death in 1816. Here was Presteigne's fashionable promenade in the days when " the fashion " came to Presteigne. G. Lipscomb, in his Journey into Wales, written in 1799, refers to a bowling green on the Warden, but this had disappeared before Williams wrote in 1818. Williams refers to " an agreeable and circuitous gravel walk, planted on each side with shrubs."†

---

* The castle mounds at Pilleth and Bryn-y-Castell at Knighton, both over 20 feet high, give a good idea of what was probably the original appearance of the Presteigne mound.
† The town once nearly lost the Warden. The story of its successful fight to retain possession is told on pp. 114-115.

The grounds around the modern house of Silia (belonging to Mrs. Hugh Lee) should be mentioned as they contain one of the finest collections of conifers in the country. Captain James Beavan (commanding the local Volunteers) spent most of his time in the 1860's and 1870's planting these trees and beautifying the grounds. He kept his own pack of hounds, and kennelled them by the cottage at the entrance to the grounds. He lived at 8, Broad Street, and replaced its picturesque Georgian bow windows with the modern frontage seen to-day, a transformation almost as bad as that of the 18th century Red House on the other side of the street.*

We might conclude this chapter with a few words about the use of the Welsh language, though, so far as Presteigne is concerned, it belongs neither to Yesterday nor to To-day. In most of the rest of Radnorshire Welsh was largely spoken up to the beginning of the 18th century, but died out rapidly in that century. In the west, around St. Harmons, it lingered until after 1870. Old farms or houses with Welsh names in the immediate neighbourhood of Presteigne are an exception, which makes it doubtful whether much Welsh was ever spoken there.

The *Frith* Wood, north of the town, however, is a relic of Welsh, the original name, no doubt, being Ffridd, meaning a woodland sheep walk. There is also a derelict house a mile beyond, which the Ordnance map calls Llys-y-wern. This is now known locally as Lice-evan; in the 17th century manor rolls of Norton it is called Lease Evor. Lease is much nearer than Lice to the Welsh pronunciation of Llys, and the change is an interesting example of the gradual corruption of Welsh names which has occurred in many parts of Radnorshire.† An example of the Welsh pronunciation persisting despite spelling changes is found in the Mynd hill, near New Radnor. The original spelling was Mynydd, pronounced Munith (soft th). By 1800 the name was spelt Mynidd, and it is now Mynd, but the y is pronounced in the old way, to give the sound Mund.

There are plenty of Welsh names to this day around Cascob, Whitton, Pilleth, and Knighton, and Lewis, writing in 1833, said that Welsh was spoken in these places " little more than a century ago." Cascob was within the Welshry of the lordship of Radnor.

---

* Every front window of this house was altered, some were removed to make room for the present doors, and the large central door, with its steps and round-headed windows above, were replaced by the present bay windows.

† At New Radnor the Bach Hill is pronounced as the Baitch Hill, and Clawdd Lane (properly Clowth, with a soft th) is called Claud Lane; and there are mixtures of the two languages, such as Bach Hill and Great Creigiau.

It is probable that all the places mentioned would make Knighton their market town, and so tend to preserve the Welsh language there. Presteigne market would get the people from Evenjobb, Kinnerton, and other places in the Englishry of the old lordship, speaking little if any Welsh. There would be some Welsh spoken in New Radnor, and it was probably universal west of that town.

The dialect of Radnorshire includes some words and phrases which are obviously of Welsh origin. This subject has been dealt with in the writer's book, " Radnor Old and New," published by the printers of this book. A glossary of over 300 words is given, of which the great majority would be known in Presteigne. A supplement to this glossary is included as an Appendix in the present book.

Mention is made in the same book of the Radnorshire way with pronouns, and the following old Radnorshire epitaph is quoted among the examples given :

Him as was has gone from we ;
Us as is must go to he.

This usage is by no means peculiar to Presteigne. So it is rather hard to explain why in former days Presteigne in particular got the nickname "Him's Town." But the fact remains, and is duly recorded here, for the satisfaction of the older generation "out for" Knighton and other places who were thus wont to indulge their wit at the expense of their county town.

XI

Festival and Feast

It is difficult for anyone who has not known Presteigne for a long lifetime, and who has not inherited the traditions of the place, to picture life there in the last century or so. It is one matter to write the history of a town in broad outline, and quite a different matter to put in the lights and shades and give a picture of its inhabitants and their amusements, interests, and occupations outside the common, daily round. We have the memories of old inhabitants to draw upon, and can learn something of events from them. But the *atmosphere* is lacking, the personalities who made the events memorable, the jollity and good humour, the noise and the confusion, taste and smell—all these have gone and their savour is lost. We can only record the events as matters of history, and the reader must be left to picture the scene—the joy and happiness of the summer day, beribboned damsels and holiday attire, the merry meetings of friends, carousals at every inn, the flush and excitement on every face.

Of such would be the fairs which enlivened Presteigne in the old days, and indeed up to 40 or 50 years ago. As we have already seen, Bishop Richard Martin bestowed two fairs upon the town in the 15th century. A Parliamentary document of 1650 gave the dates as 24th June and 29th November. In a list of 1766 the dates are given as 24th June and 30th November, and it is stated that " sheep, horned cattle and horses " were sold at both fairs. Another list of 1820 gives two fairs, with the second date as 11th December. By 1845 there were five fairs, the dates of which were 8th February, 9th May, 20th June, 13th October, and 11th December. Edward Newell, in his Almanac of 1862, gave the same five dates, except for February, which he described as the Saturday before 13th February. The last-named was known as the Candlemas Fair.

From the point of view of merriment and rowdiness, the most important fairs were those of 9th May, which was a hiring fair and came to be called the Pleasure Fair, and the oldest of all, the June fair, which from time immemorial was held on the Warden, and was known as the Warden Wake. The other fairs were more for the sale of livestock; they attracted a great many people, especially the October fair, which was also a pleasure fair.

At the May Pleasure Fair farm servants, both men and women, who wished to change masters, came into the town and stood around until a satisfactory bargain had been struck with a farmer. They received a shilling as " earnest money," and then set about the real business of the day, which was having as good a time as possible on this, their one holiday of the year. The streets of the town were filled with booths and stalls, roundabouts, etc., and there were usually performing bears and other wild animals to be seen. The inns did a roaring trade, and the liveliness increased as the day went on. Special constables were sworn in for the occasion in the old days, and later extra police were drafted into the town.

The Sessional Rolls for 1821 give a vivid little impression of the spirit of jollity abroad. The fair that year coincided with the General Sessions; so we find John Farrer committed to the county gaol " for disturbing the Court by blowing wind instruments after having been frequently admonished not to do so "; and William Jones (a boy) likewise committed for letting off crackers. (Both were released before the Court rose.)

The May fair continued up to the first year of the present war. It had long ceased to be a hiring fair, and was not the whole-hearted occasion of former years, though there were still round-abouts and side shows, and a great deal of noise.

The Warden Wake attracted a very large gathering. It was rather like Epsom Downs on Derby Day, complete with gipsy for-tune-tellers, ballad mongers, wandering minstrels, drinking booths, shooting galleries, swing boats, and other forms of entertainment. Cheap-jacks did a thriving trade, and on the refreshment stalls were vast quantities of cherries—from which fact the fair was often called the Cherry Wake. The songs of the ballad mongers were eagerly bought and learnt, for singing was a popular pastime, especially at the alehouses.

There was dancing on the green at night, to the tune of the fiddles, and a fair amount of fighting before the day ended. In the 1880's a certain policeman, named Massey, of great girth and suit-able strength, acquired considerable skill in separating combatants, with the aid of a stout ash stick. The Wake, with its old-time revelries, ceased about 1898, though the festival was observed for a few years longer, in more subdued fashion.

In the early years of the last century, up to about the 1830's, there were prize fights at the Warden Wake, which drew " the fancy " from far distances. Challenges were issued as long as 12 months beforehand, and the prize money amounted to £15 or more. Bare fists were used, of course, and men fought as long as they could see and stand. A former resident of the town, whose grandfather took part in these fights, relates that they sometimes went to 40 rounds. One of the gaolers, William Paytoe by name, was a fighter of some renown. A Dr. Pyefinch of the town was skilled at patching up combatants at the ringside. The grandfather spoke of many fights taking place in quiet spots around Presteigne, apart from the Wake affairs, just for the love of the sport, so to speak, and to settle who was best man in a particular neighbourhood.

He mentioned Kitty's Jack as the name of a well-known fighter. This form of name was probably not uncommon in those days, and seems worth mentioning as a sidelight on the times, and the open recognition of the surname difficulty in certain cases.

While on the subject of names, it might be added that Radnorshire still shares the Welsh custom of naming people in conjunction with their farms or businesses. Thus, Jones Upper House, Davies the Bryn, Powell the Baker. Christian names are used in the same way, as Ben the Mill. The old women who kept the turnpike gates were invariably known by their Christian names, and became Martha (or whatever the name was) the Turnpike.

Nicknames are still common, and are usually apt enough to make one almost forget the person's real name. On many hangs a story. A character long since passed away was universally known as " Sally rue the day." Hers was a sad story—but need it be said, so expressive is the name?

The rope-pulling, which took place on Shrove Tuesday, was a very old institution. In olden times the whole of the day was given up to games and merry-making, but only the rope-pulling survived, to take place in the evening. Most of the working-men and lads of the town joined in the fun. The rope was thrown to them from the King's Head Inn (now 44, High Street). The contest usually ended in Broad Street. It was predicted that if the people pulling down the street were able to dip the rope in the river, the price of grain would be dear that year; if the other side won, then the price would go down. There is a useful post under the old Tudor shop at the top of Broad Street which, unless the river party were watchful, greatly helped the people with a loose end of rope at the top of the street. The rope was sold after the contest, and the proceeds went largely to the inns, by way of many a thirsty throat. These Shrove Tuesday celebrations have been past history for 40 years.

Guy Fawkes Day was a recognised occasion for boisterous behaviour. It was usual to make a life-size Guy and carry him in procession to a meadow by the river, to be burnt with due ceremony. Not infrequently the Guy took the form of someone in the town who had rendered himself unpopular.

There was a special occasion on 18th November, 1884, when an effigy was carried through the town headed by a drum and fife band and followed by a crowd of three or four hundred people. The victim was the church organist, who had played the Dead March in Saul in church, to mark, it was alleged, the return from holiday of the curate, a popular person in the town, but disliked by the organist. The police sergeant and constable were removed from Presteigne for not having tried to stop the proceedings.

All Hallows Eve was an important occasion in former years. It was known as Llan Hollan's Eve in Radnorshire and the November fair at Knighton is still called Llanhollan Fair by some of the older people. All homesteads (to quote the Rev. D. Edmondes Owen) were lit with rush candles to welcome young people to indulge in games peculiar to the occasion, and the old people to narrate folk-lore stories.

Presteigne once had its own Race Meeting. This originally took place on Broad Heath Common, but in later years was sometimes held at Norton Manor. Meetings are known to have taken place at least as early as 1839.* A Hereford newspaper of 1842 records that " these races came off with great éclat on 2nd September, under the stewardship of Richard Price, whose polite demeanour was the theme of praise." The last of the meetings took place in the 1870's. Sir Richard Green-Price, of Norton Manor (who died in 1887), was a keen supporter. He also, with other members of his family, took a large part in forming a Polo Club in 1874; the games were played on Broad Heath, by the racecourse. In the 1860's and 1870's Presteigne also had an Archery Club, whose meetings were " fashionably attended."

It must be admitted that, compared with these old days, Presteigne is to-day a quiet backwater, though some allowance must be made for war-time restrictions. Even that old-time functionary, the town-crier, has disappeared since the last holder of that office (Mr. George Barrington) resigned in 1940. None of the oldest inhabitants remembers the town without a crier before this date.

The only old-time ceremony still observed is the procession of the Judge and Sheriff to and from church, before the Assizes. We can spare the public hangings which, it is to be feared, formerly attracted large crowds, as certainly did the General Sessions and Assizes, when hanging and transportation sentences were the order of the day. It is a pity, though, that the out-of-door frolics of the past have disappeared. Doubtless they were often rough and dis-

---

* The Knighton Meeting was an older institution, races taking place there in 1812, if not before that date. Kington had a race course on Bradnor Hill in 1770, its Hergest course being opened in 1826.

RADNORSHIRE ARMS HOTEL   *The Porch bears the date* 1616.

(*To face page* 64).

HEREFORD STREET—*Old Sun Inn (with upper bay window and two doors) and old Rose & Crown (white house at end).*

HEREFORD STREET—*Old Apple Tree Inn (with one bay and two doors) and a Tudor black & white house beyond.*

(To face page 65).

orderly affairs, but they provided an outlet for high spirits, and welded the community together to an extent which paler functions fail of achieving—leaving behind memories and a relish which outlived sadness and decay.

Perhaps the May Pleasure Fair will be revived after the War. There was another function which the War closed down—for the duration only, we will hope. This was the Agricultural Show, which was started in 1936 and was held each September in the field below Silia. In addition to exhibitions of horses, cattle, sheep, pigs, poultry, etc., there were pony trotting and other competitions, and sheep dog trials, which attracted large entries. The War of 1914-18 put a stop to earlier Shows of the same kind. Various competitions, including ploughing matches, had been run as far back as 1870 by a society formed about that time and called the Presteigne and Luggside Agricultural Improvement Society.

In former years also there was a Horticultural Show, which took place on August Bank Holiday. Up to 1914 it was held in the grounds of Boultibrooke, and later, with rather diminished splendour, in the field near Fold Farm. This Show was revived on August Bank Holiday, 1943, on the playing field of the County School. Sheep dog trials were also revived last year (1944).

The Horticultural Show was a gala day for the Oddfellows, who used to " walk " on that day. The Foresters held their annual " walk " and fête on 29th May (later on Whit-Monday). The Old Club (Presteigne Benefit Society, formed in 1805) " walked " to the Warden Wake, after a service in the parish church.

All these occasions were marked by festive meals at one inn or another. Nor must we forget, in a chapter on Feasts, the tenants' dinners which invariably accompanied the half-yearly Tithe Rent Audits. These continued into the present century. Different estates met at different inns (usually the Radnorshire Arms, the Duke's Arms, or the Castle), and happy functions they were, bringing landlord and tenant into a close relationship such as we can hardly imagine to-day.

Presteigne is in the country of the Radnor and West Hereford foxhounds, which frequently meet in the neighbourhood. There is also a local subscription pack of otter hounds, which for many years have visited the Lugg around Presteigne, among other places.

The Lugg is famous for its trout and grayling, and attracts many fishermen. A catch made in 1944 is worthy of record. A local enthusiast landed a trout weighing 5 lb. 10 oz. If anyone doubts, let it be added that the same is duly recorded in the Parish Magazine.

The Militia parade ground was on the left-hand side of the road beyond Lugg bridge, opposite Stapleton House. Presteigne was also the headquarters of the Radnorshire Volunteer Rifle Corps (later, in the 1870's and after, the No. 9 Company of the 1st Hereford Rifle Volunteers), and many were the Volunteer meetings and inspections which it saw. There is still at the Shire Hall the Colour presented by Lady Jane Walsh in 1861 to the Radnorshire Rifle Volunteers.

Presteigne's nearest approach to military display recently have been the parades by the local Company of the 1st Radnorshire Battalion of the Home Guard. To add to this up-to-date touch, let it be recorded that last year Presteigne saw its first (and perhaps last) baseball match, played on the County School ground by American soldiers encamped in the neighbourhood. Americans lined one side of the field, Italians from the Prisoners of War Camp near Clatterbrune the opposite side, and there was also a party of Australian airmen among the spectators. The Presteigne hills, which have seen so many " invaders," can hardly have looked down on a stranger gathering.

It is perhaps difficult to-day to think of Presteigne as a centre of fashion as well as gaiety. Yet it undoubtedly was so in the 18th century, and in much of the last century—almost a Welsh Bath, in which Jane Austen might have felt at home. Williams, in 1818, said of Presteigne, " it forms a pleasing retreat for its (the county's) gentry, and is a respectable residence for genteel families that love quiet and retirement and that can be delighted with picturesque scenery."

That they got something more than the latter is shown in the Shire Hall records. A licence was granted in December, 1790, for players " to perform operas, plays or farces as now are or hereafter shall be performed or represented in the City of Westminster " for a period of 60 days. A Mr. Willman had a licence in April, 1798, to perform plays in Presteigne for six weeks. Williams also mentions card and dancing assemblies in the winter season. Cockfighting, too, he says, was formerly "a favourite and popular diversion, pursued by gentlemen of figure and respectability."

The files of the *Hereford Journal* and *Hereford Times* contain many accounts of well-attended concerts in early Victorian times. Rather typical is the following, from the *Times* of 29th October, 1842: " Mr. Jones held his second concert in the large room of the Radnorshire Arms Hotel on Wednesday se'nnight, which was most numerously and respectably attended." Later, in 1874, we read of the Drawing Room Opera Company giving a whole week of opera at the Assembly Rooms; " Maritana " and the " Bohemian Girl " were among the works performed.

Local amateur talent did its full share in providing entertainments for the town. In the early 1860's, for instance, there was a flourishing Philharmonic Society, which gave its concerts in the public room above the old Market Hall. The Popular Penny Readings were also held at frequent intervals during the winter season in the 1860's and 1870's. They included song and piano items, recitations, etc., besides short readings and lectures. In the 1880's their place was taken by what were known as Popular Entertainments. The Penny Readings were revived for a time at a later period, and continued into the early years of this century.

The Presteigne Amateur Christy Minstrels gave concerts for many years from the early 1880's onwards. Later there was a Presteigne Musical Society, which gave at least two concerts every season, while the local amateur actors presented plays and *tableaux vivants*. We read of 60 performers taking part in these concerts in the 1890's, including an orchestra of a dozen or more. The town band is an old institution, and is still in being.

For indoor entertainment Presteigne now has cinema shows at the Assembly Rooms four nights a week, a dance usually on one of the other nights of the week, and a whist drive perhaps on the remaining night. Since this is a record of the present as well as of the past, it should be added that a Choral Society was started in the winter of 1942-3, which has already given several successful performances at the Assembly Rooms.

XII

Wayfarers and Inns

It has been jokingly remarked that every other house in Presteigne has been an inn at some time or other. If alehouses are included, we can make up a total of at least 26, which is certainly a high proportion, especially as the list omits houses which took out licences to sell beer on special occasions like the fairs.

As we have already seen, Presteigne owed some of its early importance to its being the meeting place of two main routes, one north to south, the other east to west. There were probably many occasions when the accommodation of the inns was required to the full by the travellers passing through the town. The Sessions would bring an additional number of people.

Until the stage coaches arrived (about 1780), the wayfarers who passed through Presteigne would be mostly mounted or on foot. There was hardly any wheeled traffic until the 17th century, and then it was confined chiefly to carriers' carts from Leominster and other neighbouring towns, and to the stage wagons. Goods were conveyed about the country by means of pack-horses, long trains of which would doubtless often be seen. The farmers used sledges, long carts mounted on runners.

It has to be remembered that for more than 1,200 years after the Romans left Britain (say up to 1650), very little had been done to improve the roads. In Wales up to even later the Roman roads were the only constructed roads in the country. The rest were little more than trackways, with deep ruts and long patches of thick mud (sometimes 18 inches deep), or with rocky, uneven surfaces, often pitted with holes.

A study of the prehistoric ridgeways is outside the scope of this book. Those who are interested in the subject will find several such in the neighbourhood of Presteigne. There is one, for instance, which descends from the direction of Bradnor Hill on to the Kington road, some 500 yards beyond the Rodd. Another can be seen on the high ground between Beggar's Bush and Cold Oak; this was used by wheeled traffic from Presteigne up to the 18th century, and joins another ancient track coming from Evenjobb. There is a third on the hills towards Knighton, along Reeves Lane and Llanwen Hill, crossing the Knighton road at the Rhos fingerpost.   The first of these was used by the Welsh cattle drovers, and possibly also the others.   The second probably passed Presteigne by way of Cold Harbour, the Folly, Hoarstone Lane, the Cat and Fiddle, Broad Heath, and thence across the Lugg in the direction of Limebrook and Lingen.

Parishes and landowners were supposed to look after the stretches of road that passed through their ground.   An Act of 1555 made it compulsory for every able-bodied person to give six days' gratuitous service on the roads, and this statutory labour was exacted up to the end of the 18th century, and even later in some places.*   Little was done, however, beyond scouring ditches and throwing down loads of stone and rubbish.   The Sessional Rolls at the Shire Hall record many fines on parishes for neglecting their roads, but the fines do not seem to have had much effect, as the same parishes are mentioned again and again.

Two entries in local (Norton) manor rolls seem worth quoting. In 1755 a man was fined for not filling up '' the quarries '' he had made in the high road.   Another in 1765 was presented for ''annoying the highway from Norton to Radnor by erecting a stank across it and making a deep hole in the said highway which is dangerous for passengers.''

With such hazards to be encountered, we can understand the slow rate of travel in those days.   It was a costly business, too. In 1801 the county paid a man £31 10s. for his expense and trouble in conveying two prisoners, under sentence of transportation, from Presteigne to Portsmouth.   Even as late as 1825 the return journey for a man and two assistants taking five prisoners to the hulks at Woolwich cost the county £45 18s., and occupied three weeks. These journeys were probably made by stage wagons, which were the cheapest form of transport in those days, and also the slowest. In 1844 we read of prisoners being sent by day coach.

There are other interesting sidelights on the state of the roads in the Shire Hall records.   From the bills submitted by the petty constables it appears that prisoners were usually brought to the county gaol on foot in the 18th century.   Carts would be too expensive, and probably slower.   Paupers and the like were often conveyed on horseback, sometimes riding pillion with the constable. In 1753 a constable who had to take a pauper girl 11 miles charged 7s. for the journey and 1s. 6d. for the keep of himself and his horse one night.   There is an order of 1764 for a blind old pauper woman with a legal settlement in Merionethshire to be conveyed on horseback to the first town on a direct road in the next county.

---

* The number of days' labour exacted gradually lessened, but the obligation remained until the Highways Act of 1835 became law.

A printed tariff was issued in 1819 showing the mileage rates payable to petty constables for conveying "vagabonds and incorrigible rogues"; for one vagrant on foot they could charge 3d. a mile, for two 4d., while, if on horseback, the charges were 6d. a mile for one, 8d. for two; a cart could be used for three or more, at 1s. a mile.

Presteigne was on the main route from London to Aberystwyth up to 1780 or 1790. A service of stage wagons was plying on this route from the 17th century. The road beyond Presteigne went through Discoed and Cascob, and thence in a fairly straight line over the hills to Rhayader, passing south of Llanddewi. Some of it is hardly traceable to-day, and much of it must have made very rough going.

These old stage wagons were on the roads up to the end of the 18th century, and even later. They were long, lumbering vehicles, devoid of springs, with wide wheels to help them over the mud, and were mostly used by the poorer people, carrying 30 or 40. They had six horses, and their average rate of travel was two miles an hour, or 20 miles a day. The driver was forbidden to drive from the wagon for fear of his falling asleep, so he walked, or rode an extra horse at the head of the team.

The construction of the turnpike roads and the engineering skill of men like Telford and Macadam revolutionised travel in the latter part of the 18th century. By 1780 or soon after Presteigne had two turnpike roads passing through it, one connecting Leominster with New Radnor, and the other Kington with Knighton. Williams says the latter went into the parish of Bleddfa and turned right just short of Mynachty.* This would make the route much longer than the present one, and also than the old road over Stonewall Hill. We know that some parts of these roads, if not the whole, were open in 1790, as there were turnpike gates at Presteigne, Nash, Stapleton, Corton, and Broad Heath, which were let for a total sum of £168 that year. It would be about this time that the old road past the Slough to Evenjobb and Beggar's Bush fell largely into disuse, to form the present green tracks.

About the same period the turnpike through Kington and New Radnor to Rhayader and Aberystwyth was opened, and became the main coaching road from Gloucester to Aberystwyth. The Worcester-Aberystwyth coaches came through Presteigne, proceeding to New Radnor by way of Discoed, Beggar's Bush and Kinnerton. These coaches were certainly still running in 1814, as they are mentioned in Cary's Travelling Companion of that year. At a later date they were diverted from Presteigne to Kington.

---

* The turnpike through Bleddfa to Penybont was not opened until 1837.

We do not know the date of this change. It was probably 1821, up to which year Kington got its London letters through Presteigne. They were then delivered by "horse post", but formerly the postman walked the 14 miles to Kington and back, delivering each letter himself. It would be something of a blow to Presteigne, though the gentry were more or less unaffected, as they could, and did, drive their own carriages to Worcester (to proceed by coach to London). By 1826 the general public were able to get to Worcester again by the Royal Radnor coach, which left the Castle Inn at 6 a.m., except on Saturday market day, when it left at 4 a.m.

The Aberystwyth coaches came again to Presteigne in 1833. The *Hereford Times* of that year advertised a " New Patent Safety Coach," called the Prince of Wales, which ran by way of Presteigne on its journey from Worcester to Aberystwyth, in competition with the coaches using the Kington road. This changed horses at the Radnorshire Arms and proceeded by Beggar's Bush through New Radnor. Passengers to London stayed the night at Worcester, where they caught the Aurora day coach next day.

Next year (1834) this coach started at Cheltenham instead of Worcester. It left the Plough, Cheltenham, at 6 a.m., was at Ledbury at 8.30, Leominster at 11, Presteigne at 1 p.m., Llandegley at 3 p.m., Cross Gates at 3.30, Rhayader at 5, and the Talbot, Aberystwyth at 9.p.m. This service was supplemented in 1835 by another coach, called the Owen Glendower, which left Birmingham at 6.15 a.m., and by way of Stourbridge, Tenbury, Leominster, and Presteigne, proceeded to Llandrindod Wells and Aberystwyth, which it reached at 8.30 p.m. The turnpike gates around Presteigne, which were let for £168 in 1790, fetched £379 in 1837—sure evidence of the increased traffic of the roads.

At this period most of the inns would have changes of horses for travellers, and some form of conveyance, including certainly the Radnorshire Arms, Duke's Arms, the New Inn (now the Posting House Garage), the Castle Inn, and the Oxford Arms. A very different state of affairs from 20 or 30 years back. A writer of about 1803 said that there was then only one public carriage in the whole of Radnorshire, which was a postchaise kept at Rhayader— illustrative, the writer added, " of the retirement to which the natives of these mountains are doomed." By 1810 post horses were also kept at Penybont, and in 1812 Llandegley Wells (then a fashionable watering place) was advertising "neat postchaises, careful drivers, and able horses."

The railways spread rapidly through Radnorshire in the 1860's and 1870's, and the stage coaches disappeared. The turnpikes and toll gates persisted some years longer. Some old inhabitants still refer to the main roads as the "turnpikes." They were finally taken over by the County Councils under the Local Government Act of 1888.

Several of the turnpike houses around Presteigne are still standing. They are (1) the small house some 300 yards beyond the Lugg bridge, on the right-hand side of the Stapleton road; (2) the house in High Street at the corner of Warden Lane (to which a storey was added, after its turnpike days); (3) the cottage near Corton, at the junction of the Kington and Walton roads; (4) the cottage at the Nash turning, on the Kington road. There were gates at all these points. There was a gate just short of the turning for Knighton; parts of the wall of the house may still be seen, on the left as you leave Presteigne. Another gate stood by the County School; its house was on the opposite corner of the road leading over the railway bridge.*

There are many references in the Sessional Rolls before 1888 to the various bridges in the county, which were the special care of the county magistrates. At most General Sessions some bridge or other was reported to be "ruinous" or "out of repair," and their condition must have added considerably to the hazards of the roads. Even in 1885, when a Builth man wished to use a traction engine on the county roads, the surveyors reported that none of the bridges or road arches would stand the weight of such a vehicle.

A railway poster of 1868 shows that Presteigne had then a daily omnibus service to Knighton. It connected with the train leaving Knighton at 10 a.m. for Craven Arms and Shrewsbury, returning to Presteigne after the arrival of the return train, due at Knighton at 3 p.m. By this means Presteigne people got nearly 2½ hours at Shrewsbury. The omnibus, by the way, was a one-horse affair, taking six passengers at a squeeze, who had to walk up Hares Green pitch and other steep parts of the road. Many preferred to get out and walk *down* some of the hills, for safety's sake!

At the present time (1945) war-time restrictions still permit of four buses daily between Presteigne and Knighton, but have cut down the other services to three days a week to Leominster and Kington, and two days to Hereford, while there are but two trains a day (compared with three before the War).

Before leaving the subject of the roads and their users, mention should be made of a stage coach revival which took place for

---

* The offices of the Radnorshire Turnpike Trust were in the Georgian brick building (now a butcher's shop) opposite the Castle Inn.

a short period in the later 1870's and early 1880's. This was brought about by Captain Cecil Otway, a generous benefactor of Presteigne and the county. Captain Otway drove the coach himself and provided the horses. He first ran a service from Kington to Llandrindod, and replaced this next year by one from Presteigne to Aberystwyth.

The coach started at the Duke's Arms, proceeding by way of Knill and Walton to New Radnor, and so on to Rhayader and Aberystwyth. The coach left Presteigne at 10.5 a.m., and was due at Aberystwyth at 6 p.m.; the return journey took 25 minutes less. Return fares for the whole journey were 30s. outside, 25s. inside. The service, for the summer months only, and starting from each place alternate days, became widely known and was well patronised. Forty horses were stationed along the route to make the change-overs.

The " inns " of Presteigne almost need a chapter of their own. Several have already been mentioned in connection with wayfarers. Doubtless most of the others catered for their comfort. At the time Captain Otway ran his coach, the Duke's Arms, in Broad Street, was perhaps the most fashionable in the town, as to-day the Radnorshire Arms might claim that position. The Radnorshire Arms, with its porch bearing the date 1616, its chimneys and some other parts of the same date, and general " black and white " appearance (though some of this is a reconstruction of the last century), is one of the most picturesque hotels in Wales. In the earlier part of the 19th century some of the town's concerts were held here, instead of in the room over the market hall, in which most such functions then took place. The stables, used in the old coaching days, were opposite the hotel, where is now the garage.

The Duke's Arms has preserved a good deal of 17th century and even earlier work, and is said to have started its career as an inn in the 15th century. It has an open gallery behind, and a large upstairs room, which must have seen many a festive table; this room was used for political meetings as well as other popular functions.* The inn has a board bearing the arms of the Duke of Chandos. As this title was only created in 1719, the inn probably had a different name originally. A letter from a Parliamentary Commissioner at Presteigne in 1652 asked for correspondence to be sent by the Leominster carrier to the Talbot. It is possible that this was the original name of the Duke's Arms. No other inn in the town is known to have had that name, which was a popular one in the district, Knighton, Kington and Leominster each having a Talbot.

---

* The Marquis of Hartington, M.P. for Radnor Boroughs, addressed a meeting here in May, 1873.

Before the present Shire Hall was opened in 1830, it was a common procedure for the county magistrates, after disposing of prisoners, to adjourn to an inn to discuss the rest of their business. The bills for their dinners among the Sessional Rolls point to some improvement of the occasion. The houses patronised included the two already mentioned, and also the Castle and the Rose and Crown. The Castle, still standing in High Street, is a 17th century building; both the Castle and the Duke's Arms had bowling alleys. The Rose and Crown, part of which still exists, was on the present site of Lloyd's Bank in Hereford Street; it was an important inn in the 18th century and early 19th century.

The present-day licensed houses, in addition to the Radnorshire Arms, Duke's Arms, and the Castle, are : in *St. David's Street,* the Bull; in *Scottleton Street,* the Royal Oak (known as the Top Oak, to distinguish it from the Oak which was formerly open in Broad Street); in *Hereford Street,* the Farmer's Arms, the Oxford Arms, and the Barley Mow. All these were included in a list of licensed premises of 1823, with the exception of the Farmers' Arms. The attractive Bull has always had its vogue ; it was here that the town celebrated with a dinner the marriage of Queen Victoria in 1840.

And, finally, for the inns and beerhouses which have ceased to exist as such, though the buildings remain, except that of the Lion. First, in *Broad Street,* there were the Blue Boar (now number 10) and the Oak (still the Old Oak House), both of which were beerhouses, and existed in the 17th century; there was also the Bridge Inn (now Ford View, the old house next to the bridge). In *High Street,* there were the Red Lion (now 46), and after that was closed, the Lion at 41 (burnt down in 1906); the King's Head (now 44); the New Inn, facing St. David's Street; the Globe, at the corner of Chapel Terrace; also the Queen's Head and the George, the sites of which the writer has been unable to identify. All these, except the Bridge Inn, the Globe, and the Lion, were named in a list of 1828.

In *Scottleton Street,* there was the Bell (now numbers 2 and 3). In *Hereford Street* there were, besides the Rose and Crown already mentioned, the Sun (now Millfields printing premises);* the Apple Tree (now 47); the Masons' Arms beerhouse (now 14); the Machine House beerhouse (now 9, at the corner of Back Lane). In *Green End* there was the Fountain (now number 1). The Grove, first house on the right across the Lugg bridge, was another inn, which may be included in our Presteigne list, though on the Hereford side of the river.

---

* The Sun had a large room upstairs, capable of seating 150 people or more. Here the tradesmen of the town and their families met in 1866 to celebrate the opening of the new Market Hall.

This makes a total of eight houses at present licensed, and 18 others licensed at some time or other in, say, the last 120 years, 26 in all.

Most of the public, and not a few of the private, houses brewed their own beer up to the 1870's, and some of the inns later than that. In 18th century advertisements of private houses in Presteigne to be let, we find a brewhouse with furnace as one of the attractions (with such items as sashed windows, " commodious " garrets, and wainscotted parlours). Warden Court had a malt house.

There were heavy penalties for any publican who used " pernicious ingredients," such as " sugar, honey, foreign grains, Guinea pepper, the liquor called *effentia bine,* made from malt and water boiled up," or who used broom or wormwood or any other bitter ingredient instead of hops. A regulation of the time of Queen Elizabeth laid down that " all brewers that brew ale to sell shall brew good ale and wholesome for a man's body at 3d. a gallon and 1d. a gallon, to be warranted by the ale taster."

The Present Practice of a Justice of the Peace, published in 1790, which tells of the penalties for unscrupulous brewers, also describes the penalties for a person who " continues drinking or tipling " in any inn or alehouse or who is convicted of drunkenness. First offenders in the former case were to be fined 3s. 4d., to be paid to the churchwardens for the use of the poor; failing payment, they were to be set in the stocks for four hours. Drunkards were to pay a fine of 5s., or to be set in the stocks for six hours. The penalties were increased if the offence was repeated, and " all constables, churchwardens, aleconners, and sidesmen in their several and respective oaths incident to their office " were charged to prevent such offences. An alehouse keeper convicted of being drunk was " utterly disabled " from keeping an alehouse for three years.

It is to be feared that there was a time-lag between the abolition of some of the inns and the disappearance of the wayfarers who once filled them, and that the tiplers prevailed for a time. The Chief Constable made constant complaints in the 1880's that there were too many inns and beerhouses. Even in 1904 Presteigne still had 14 such premises, while Knighton had 16. Perhaps it is a natural reaction from those days which has recently led the " city fathers " of Presteigne to oppose the grant of even one off-licence for the town. Certainly Presteigne is a far more sober place to-day than it was 40—even 30—years ago.

XIII

The Parish Church

R. Alun Roberts in " Welsh Home-Spun," writing of the Welsh peasantry in the 15th century, says " Their existence was in no way despicable. Their lives were closely bound up with Nature, and their religion was not constantly divorced from their daily life. Life was corporate and closely knit within the confines of the parish, and the church figured tremendously in it all . . ." " With the rise of the Tudors . . . the blight [of the new landlords] was most heavily visited on the peasantry . . . poverty developed apace."

That seems a very true picture of the course of events. Not that we can blame the Church altogether. The Reformation was bound to come, but it brought a new landed class into power, who thrived on their ill-gotten spoils of Church land and property, and the new pastors of the people were too often powerless to protect their flocks. Men lost heart and the Church suffered. The Puritan revival of the 17th century gave way to the apathy of the 18th century, which was checked only by movements which led away from the Church of England. The Oxford Movement of the early 19th century brought people's minds back to the early ideals of the Reformation and restored much which the Church had lost. But the recovery cannot be said to have been more than partial, and though we speak of the clergy still as a class apart, and do not include the ministers of the Free Churches in that term, their sway is limited in the main to their own congregations, as much as is that of the " ministers " to theirs.

So we give a separate chapter to the parish church of Presteigne for the interest of its history, rather than for any particular prominence it now has in the life of the town, which is the main subject of this book.

The ecclesiastical parish of Presteigne covers the huge area of 11,428 acres, though its population at the Census of 1931 was only 1,587. It includes the civil parishes of Presteigne and Discoed, in Radnorshire, and in Herefordshire takes in Stapleton, Willey and Lower Kinsham, Combe, and Rodd, Nash and Little Brampton. Discoed forms a Chapelry within the parish. It is probable that some of the other places formed separate chapelries before the

Reformation. The Baptists have a church at Ackhill, and another at Stansbatch (which is served from Presteigne). The Methodists have churches (also served from Presteigne) at Willey, Combe Moor, and Shobdon.

Under the Welsh Church Act, 1914, which became operative in 1920, border parishes part only of which were in Wales or Monmouthshire were to be treated, for the purposes of the Act, as wholly outside, or wholly inside, Wales or Monmouthshire, according to the general wishes of the inhabitants. Presteigne decided to be outside Wales, and accordingly remained in the diocese of Hereford and retained its not inconsiderable endowments, which make it one of the best livings in the diocese. Kelly's Directory of 1926 gave the net annual income as £1,265, and Crockford, 1939, as £1,026. The latter amount is equivalent to three times the standard stipend (£340) for an incumbent of the Church in Wales.

Looking at the church from the outside, standing first at the west end, then at the east end, we get an impression of two entirely different churches. This is because at the west end we see only the work of the Decorated style of the 14th century (except for the inserted 15th century windows), while at the east end we are looking mainly at the Perpendicular work of the 15th or early 16th century. These two styles comprise the greater part of the existing chuch, and the distinction between them can be seen in the colour of the stonework. The tower belongs to the 14th century building, with a window of the next century inserted in the lower storey on the south side. It formerly was surmounted by a cupola at one corner and pinnacles at the other three; these were removed in 1891. The base of the parish cross will be noticed by the tower. The cross was apparently standing in 1652, as a letter of that year refers to posting up a notice on Presteigne Cross.*

The figure in a niche above the west window appears to be a " Majesty " of Norman date. The stone base of the old vestry, now removed, will be noticed on the north side of the church. A small aperture will be noticed low down at the east end, which may have belonged to an anchorite's chamber. On the three buttresses of the south aisle are medallions which formerly contained the arms of (1) Ferrers of Chartley; (2) Townshend; (3) Ferrers of Groby and Tamworth. Only the centre medallion now has arms, which are a modern insertion of the Mortimer arms instead of the Townshend arms.

There is a tradition that the south aisle was built by Walter Devereux, Earl of Ferrers, who was Chief Justice of South Wales in the reign of Henry VIII, and was executed in 1554. The arms

---

* Published in Old Wales, Vol. 2, p. 258.

mentioned are those of branches of his family, which claimed connection with the old Lords Marchers families of Mortimer and de Braose. He was lay rector of Presteigne, and if the tradition is correct, as it may well be, we can put the date of the south aisle, and perhaps the chancel, too, at about 1500-20; the Lady Chapel was built slightly later than the south aisle.

By far the best account of the church is that given in the illustrated booklet compiled by Mr. A. M. Wilson, of Middlemoor, who specially obtained the opinion of expert architects. According to this, there were three churches before the present one, as follows:

(a) Saxon, probably 9th century: remains to be seen in north wall, portion of arch in east wall of north aisle and another in west wall of same aisle, marking the main entrance. This church would consist of a single nave and chancel, and would be about 18 feet wide.

(b) Norman church of 12th century: only remains are two round pillars at the west end of the north arcade, which are probably not in their original positions, but were built into the next church.

(c) Early English church of 13th century: portions of two arches remain, one to be seen above the pulpit, the other about half-way up the south side of the west window. It is probable that this church had no aisle, but was rather wider than the previous churches.

This brings us to the present church, of which some description has already been given from the outside. We might put the date of the nave and north aisle, with the chancel arch, at about 1320-30, and the lower part of the walls of the chancel were also probably constructed at that period. The large west window and the three windows of the north aisle belong to the period of the chancel, Lady Chapel, and south aisle, which, as already stated, may be put at about 1500-20.

The present south aisle took the place of a narrower one, which was probably similar to the north aisle; the clerestory windows of this aisle are now *inside* the church. Presteigne was but a village when this fourteenth century church was built, and it does not compare with some of the neighbouring Herefordshire churches of the same period: the nave walls, for instance, seem too high in proportion to the width and, judging from the size of the clerestory windows, the light was hardly enough for such a long nave. At the same time, the church, like Old Radnor, was far more English than Welsh in its conception, lending colour to the tradition that it was built by Roger Mortimer (who was executed by Edward III in 1230).

Presteigne had become a town of some importance when the later portions were added, and the beautiful chancel with its fine timbered roof, and the hardly less beautiful Lady Chapel and south aisle (with its original tie-beam roof), are worthy monuments for any town.

Among the ancient interior features which should be noticed, in addition to those already mentioned, are the rood loft stairs, the " squints " north and south of the chancel arches, the restored 14th century sepulchral slab in the north wall, the fragments of good 15th or early 16th century glass in the upper window of the Lady Chapel, and the traces of fresco work on the north wall of the nave arcade.

The fine tapestry hanging on the north wall is Flemish, of the early 16th century. It was presented to the church in 1737 by Richard Owen, of Little Brampton. The Colours above the chancel arch, which were presented in 1884, are those of the old Radnor Militia. Colonel G. Drage thinks they belonged to the Local Militia of 1808-16, but mentions a local tradition that they are those of the Royal Radnor Regular Militia, and saw service overseas in the 18th century. The two brass candelabra at the west end of the church are of 18th century date. The picture of the Crucifixion on the east wall of the north aisle was the gift in recent times of the Misses Coates, of the Broad Heath.

The tapestry, which depicts Christ's entry into Jerusalem on the foal of an ass, deserves more than a passing word, for it is of unique interest and beauty, and of great value. It was used as an altarpiece until 1891, when it was placed in a rough frame and hung high up at the west end of the south aisle. Here it stayed for nearly 40 years, exposed to the light and heat of the sun. At length in 1929 it was " discovered " (thanks to the late Mrs. G. Drage) by the authorities of the Victoria and Albert Museum, who were not a little amazed to find such a treasure previously unknown to them. They advised immediate treatment to prevent further deterioration. Mr. A. M. Wilson stepped in—and the thing was done, and the present frame added. The tapestry remained on exhibition at South Kensington for some little time. It is believed to be one of a series designed for Canterbury Cathedral, which was eventually (during the Commonwealth) acquired by the cathedral at Aix-en-Provence, where the whole series may still be seen. The Presteigne panel has some repair work, done when it was first woven, and it is conjectured that this led to its rejection at Canterbury, and its subsequent replacement. How it afterwards wandered into the possession of Richard Owen is a Canterbury Tale which will never be told.

There have been three important restorations in modern times. The first of these was in 1855 when (quoting Mr. Wilson's book) " the beautiful pillars of the nave were cleaned of their plaster and whitewash . . . galleries which occupied the arches of the north aisle were removed, and a large gallery (called the Stapleton gallery), which completely covered and hid the Lady Chapel, was swept away, revealing the pillars and arches between the Lady Chapel and the chancel."

The next restoration, in 1891, was carried through under the direction of J. A. Pearson. The present stone pulpit was erected, chairs were substituted for pews,* a new heating apparatus installed, and, chief among the various improvements effected, the teak screen which crosses the church was erected, in memory of Thomas Pugh and Sophia Evans, two generous benefactors of Presteigne. The previous screen was destroyed in the 16th century at the Reformation.

In 1927 was begun the restoration of the chancel, both inside and out, under the direction of Messrs. Nicholson and Clarke, of Hereford. The plaster which had covered the roof and walls was removed, and the beautiful timbering of the roof revealed, while the exterior stonework was restored and completed, parapets and pinnacles being added to take the place of those which had disappeared.

The fine three-manual organ was given to the church in 1928 by Mr. A. M. Wilson, who also endowed a fund for the stipend of the organist.† The county historian (Williams) would like to have heard its tones. He pleaded for a like position of the organ in 1818, which was then, he wrote, " at the west extremity of the church, in a situation extremely injudicious, which conceals this noble and animating instrument from the sight of the greatest part of the congregation."

Presteigne has been fortunate in its restorers, and there are few churches which have so successfully shorn themselves of the accretions of recent centuries, to bring back the splendour of the past. The mid-19th century glass in its east window is its only misfortune, and this has some colours which tone down its crudities to the

---

* In the 17th century and for many years later it was customary for each house in the parish to have its own pews or sittings, and the term "pews and kneelings" appears in old indentures as a part of the "property" transferred. It was usual for men and women to sit in separate pews, the men in front, the women behind, or else on opposite sides.

† The writer has to take responsibility for publishing this fact, but feels it should be recorded, as also the gift to the town in 1937 by the same donor of a Children's Playing Field and the Council housing site nearby.

point of toleration. It was put in at the cost of Mrs. Evans (*see* above), to the memory of a brother, and is said to be the work of a local builder, Mr. William Davies. The two stained glass figures in the window west of the font were intended to be part of the same window, but got crowded out. They were in Greenfields School for a time.

In particular the church has escaped the monumental sculptures of the 18th century, from which Old Radnor church, its only rival in Radnorshire, is not entirely free. To show how popular these sculptures were in their time, and Presteigne's fortunate escape in this respect, we might conclude this chapter with another quotation from Williams. Writing of one of the Old Radnor monuments, he says: " Beneath stands a statue of most admirable elegance of form and expression of feature, as big as life, embracing and weeping over a funereal urn. This piece of sculpture is esteemed by competent judges to equal in symmetry of form, elegance of workmanship, and liveliness of expression the best that Westminster Abbey contains."

XIV

Parish Gleanings

The Bells. There is an old jingle about the bells of Presteigne church which is quoted in Mrs. E. M. Leather's interesting book on the Folk-Lore of Herefordshire. It runs as follows:

> Up the reen and down the ridge,
> Say the bells at Pembridge;
> Up the ridge and down the reen,
> Say the bells of Presteigne.

The sound of the Presteigne bells travels over many a ploughed field, and a very beautiful peal they are, whether they go up or down the " reen "—worth going far to hear. There were six bells when this rhyme was first sung, made at the famous Gloucester foundry of Abraham Rudhall in the year 1717. The same six still peal, but two trebles were added in 1906, when the great tenor (14 cwt.) was re-cast. The present clock replaced an older one in 1838; it strikes the hours on the tenor bell. As far back as 1725 the bells rang chimes, and not until about 10 years ago (1935) did they fail to play their hymn tunes at the hours of 3 and 9 (the apparatus having got out of order).

There is a pre-Reformation bell at Heyop, which the Rev. J. T. Evans thought may have belonged originally to Presteigne.* It has the inscription, " Sce Andrea ora pro nobis."

Like all the other church bells in the country, the Presteigne bells were silent for nearly three years during the present war, from June, 1940, until Easter, 1943, when they were again permitted to ring. Old inhabitants remember a time when the bells were silent for another reason. This happened in 1891-92, because the ringers demanded more pay (asking £6 a year for half-an-hour's ringing Sunday mornings and evenings). Matters were righted before the end of 1892, and then a sad accident occurred, one of the ringers (George Vaughan) being killed in the belfry; he had gone to do some repairs to the bells, which had been left at the dangerous position of " set," and was hit by two of the bells, which he accidentally pulled down.

---

* *See* " The Church Plate of Radnorshire."

The curfew has been rung at Presteigne for nearly 400 years, but it has ceased to do so since the present war started owing to the difficulty of finding a ringer. John Beddoes, who founded the Grammar School, provided for " an able person to ring a bell every morning for ever between the feast of All Saints and the Purification of Our Lady, by the space of one half-hour, which should be called the Day Bell, and also should nightly for ever ring one other peal with the same bell at every eight of the clock, as well in summer as winter time, by the space of one half-hour, which should be called Curfew." He gave a meadow the rent of which was to pay the ringer; it is the last meadow on the right approaching Rock Bridge from Presteigne, and is still known as the Bell Meadow.

In modern times the " Day Bell " was rung all the year round, at 5 a.m. in the summer and 6 a.m. in the winter, and the curfew always at 8 p.m., but for five minutes, and not half an hour. The last ringer was Mr. Pryce Wozencroft, who died at the age of 84 in 1943.

In medieval times fires had to be extinguished when the curfew was rung. Later—and perhaps this applied to Presteigne—it was the signal for people to leave the ale houses, and not to haunt the streets without sufficient excuse.

The Graveyard. There was formerly a lych gate at the south entrance; part of the supporting walls may still be seen. It was a picturesque affair, with a tiled pointed roof. A tablet still to be seen under the ivy on the higher wall bears the inscription : " Opus Johannis Robinson. Lignum ut inveni saxum reliqui. Anno 1710." (The work of John Robinson. Where I found wood, I left stone. In the year 1710.)

Unfortunately the gate was removed at the restoration of 1891. Plans were prepared to replace it as a War Memorial after the war of 1914-18, but the idea had to be dropped, through the opposition of some of those who were not connected with the parish church, and the present Memorial in front of the County School was erected instead.

The graveyard sustained another loss by the removal in 1938 of a fine avenue of chestnut trees which lined the north wall. It was thought by some that the trees were unsafe. Williams wrote of a " grand avenue of fine sycamore trees " which " lately flourished" (1818) along the same walk, and which had been " felled and sold by an avaricious rector." Some such avenue, though it might darken the church and surrounding houses, might help to improve the present forlorn appearance of the churchyard, the neglect of which may be attributed to war-time conditions. The graveyard was cleaned in 1891, when the church was restored, and rose-trees and shrubs were planted. It will be noticed that only one old yew-tree remains, near the road on the south side of the church.

The Church House, which stands near the site of the lych gate, though a building only of the 18th century, may have a very much earlier origin. A writer in the Archæological Journal (Vol. 40) says that " near the churchyard wall, usually indeed forming a part of it, but sometimes within the enclosure and sometimes without, stood the Church House." This very well fits the Church House of Presteigne, which appears to be one of the few parishes which has preserved the ancient title.*

*Nearly every parish had its Church House in medieval times. It was the storehouse for the property of the church and parish, and was the parish hall where meetings took place and such festivities as the Parish Ales were held. It was not a dwelling place for the clergy, but the common possession of the parishioners. The Reader's House at Ludlow is believed to be one of the few Church House buildings still standing ; others are at Lincoln and Dereham.

Graves and Gravestones. There is an unusually large number of 18th century gravestones, besides many of the 19th century. Recent stones are conspicuous by their absence, as all burials have for some years been made in the cemetery under the Frith Wood (opened in 1869). Many of the stones have epitaphs, with praise for the dead or warning for the living. The following (of 1831) belongs to the former class, though one feels in some doubt as to its meaning :

> His God sustained him in the final hour;
> His final hour brought Glory to his God.

This second example (1850) conveys a message to the living :

> While pity prompts the rising sigh,
> O may this truth, imprest
> With awful power, " I, too, must die,"
> Sink deep in every heart.

That is a mild form of admonition compared with one contained in some lines on a stone of 1676 in the porch of Shobdon church, which read :

> This brave young man had all this life could give,
> And since's he's dead, canst thou presume to live?
> From death, nor wit, nor youth, nor Art can save,
> Go, Reader, and prepare thee for thy grave.

---

* Gladestry is another Radnorshire parish with a Church House near the churchyard.

Presteigne has also an example of the '' witty'' form of epitaph in the following, which is to the memory of a youth who died from a horse's kick in 1823. Surely cheerful resignation could not go further.

> My death so suddenly and quick,
> Occasion'd by a horse's kick;
> My Parents dear do not Repent
> My soul so quick to heaven was sent.

This, to a deceased gaoler (the Paytoe mentioned on page 63), who died in 1844:

> Oh, silent grave, to thee I trust
> This precious pearl of worthy dust,
> And keep it safe, oh, sacred tomb,
> Until a Wife shall ask for room.

Alas, poor Paytoe sleeps alone, and somewhere else his Wife doth moan!

There is a stone about 20 yards west of the west entrance to the memory of a sergeant of the Cameron Highlanders (Thomas Burchlate), who '' served in Egypt, Peninsula, and Waterloo, and was engaged in upwards of thirty Battles, Sieges, and Skirmishes.'' He died in 1850. The deaths are recorded of two other old soldiers at Presteigne both of whom survived their campaigns only to perish in the snow, one in 1786, the other in 1798. They are probably not the only victims of Radnorshire winters who are buried in the churchyard, for people have been lost and died in the snow around Radnor Forest, even in modern times.

Many '' felons '' have been executed at Presteigne, but they appear only exceptionally to have been buried in the churchyard. There are entries in the church registers of two horse stealers, one executed in 1785, the other in 1788. Some 12 yards to the west of the church tower there is a plain oblong headstone in memory of Mary Morgan, a girl of 17, who was hanged in 1805 for killing her new-born baby. When the grave was first made, that part of the churchyard was unconsecrated ground.

The story of this girl is told on pp. 116-117. The inscription on the stone refers to the '' young and beautiful '' girl, who was '' roused to a just shame of guilt and remorse by the eloquent and humane exertions of her benevolent Judge, Mr. Justice Hardinge.'' There is a small stone opposite the larger one, which leaves out the moral lesson of the latter, and merely says, '' He that is without sin among you, let him first cast a stone at her.''

During the 17th century most of the burials appear to have taken place in the church, though it is to be hoped this did not extend to the plague victims. There is an entry by a rector of

1699 in the church register giving rather disturbing information about the number of people buried under the altar.* Perhaps the most interesting person who has a memorial in the church is the local artist, Joseph Murray Ince, who died in 1859. The register records the burial of a Radnorshire poet, Morgan Elfael by name, who died at Presteigne in 1563.

The Church Registers. The first mandate for keeping registers of baptisms, marriages and burials was issued by Thomas Cromwell in 1538. It was not enforced very rigorously, but in 1597 it was ordained that parchment registers should be kept by every parish, and entries transcribed thereto from 1558 where possible. The Presteigne registers start at 1561, and are the earliest in Radnorshire.

The quotations from them previously made in this book chiefly concern burials. Some of the older entries are of a historical or testamentary nature. For instance, there is an account of the visit of Charles I to the parish, and of the alienation of the tithes during the time of the Commonwealth; and there is the copy of an agreement (part of it is missing) of 1653 to keep the church " dry and well tyled, with leads that likewise thereunto belong."

The parson of the 1660's appears to have been chiefly concerned about getting his tithes on fallage of wood, because Thomas Cornewall had refused to pay tithes on wood of over 20 years' growth, though losing a lawsuit in the matter. This careful worthy kept a record of every fallage and the amount of tithe paid, no doubt thinking the matter as important as any birth or burial.

An interesting entry on the fly leaf of the Burial side of book 4 reads as follows: " The Right Rev. Dr. John Butler, Bishop of Hereford, confirmed about 500 persons at Presteigne church on Wednesday, the 24th June, 1789. It was a very disagreeably rainy morning, otherwise many more would certainly have offered themselves for Confirmation. The preceding day the Bishop confirmed about 600 persons at Kington."

Confirmations in those days, and even much later, tended to take on the nature of a beanfast, and in some English rural districts, at any rate, they became repetitive affairs for not a few of those who attended them. The reference to the weather makes one rather suspicious about the Presteigne ceremony. In the 1880's and 1890's, when Churchmanship was far stronger in the parish than it is to-day, the number of Presteigne candidates for Confirmation (excluding outside parishes) usually varied from about 30 to 50.

---

* Up to the end of the 18th century most people were buried only in a shroud, the body being lifted from the coffin or shell, provided by the parish, at the edge of the grave.

Church Ornaments. When Williams wrote his County History the Church possessed two salvers of silver-gilt and " a large handsome chalice," which were presented by Thomas Owen in 1706. The Rev. H. L. Kewley, who was rector from 1898 to 1940, told the author of the Church Plate of Radnorshire that this old plate had been sold by one of his predecessors. Williams would no doubt have said what he thought about such a person. The church did not afterwards possess a proper chalice until 1893.

There is still an old silver paten, which was probably the cover of the above chalice; and a fine silver tankard flagon, bearing the hall-mark of 1692, which was given by Littleton Powell of Stanage. The present chalice and paten were used for the first time on Christmas Day, 1893. The Chapelry of Discoed shares with Rhulen the distinction of having the earliest chalice and paten in the county, both vessels dating from 1576. Of the other three Elizabethan chalices remaining in the county, two are at places near Presteigne, viz., Norton and Bleddfa ; the third is at Cregrina.

According to the Report of the Chantry Commissioners of 1548, Presteigne church had at that time no less than " four payres of vestmentes of silke with there ornaments." Needless to say, these soon disappeared after the Commissioners had made their report.

Chantry and other Services. Each of the above " payres of vestmentes " was used for one of the Chantry services, of which Presteigne had four, an unusually large number for Wales, and more than there were in any other church in the county. The Commissioners gave the names of these services, the value of the land and tenements left for their upkeep, and the names of the priests who served them. The services were: (1) St. David's; (2) Our Lady of Pity; (3) Our Lady of Grace; and (4) the Trinity. There is a tradition that the parishioners always claimed as their own the Lady Chapel at the end of the south aisle of the church, in which one or other of these services doubtless took place.

It is interesting to note that as late as 1544 Morice ap Lellowe directed in his will that two obits were to be kept yearly in the parish church of Presteigne, one obit one month after the feast of St. Michael the Archangel, the other one month after the feast of the Annunciation, for the soul of " Maister John Shurley and all Christian Souls."

Such services and the ceremonial which attended them were forgotten for centuries. Even in 1882 the *Hereford Times* recorded of an Easter service at Presteigne, that the church was entirely devoid of all external manifestations of Easter joy, " not the slightest attempt at beautifying the sacred edifice being put forth." It is happily far otherwise to-day. There is a vase of flowers on the wooden Communion Table of 1666 in the north aisle, which is tended Sunday by Sunday by some ladies long connected with the church, and which, to the writer, appears one of the most beautiful objects in the church, so choice are the flowers and so well are they arranged.

In 1893 the Rev. R. Howard Cuthbert (of All Saints', Clifton) became rector, and brought to the church, probably for the first time since the Reformation, Catholic teaching and practice. It was he who revived, after long centuries, the Dedication Festival of the Church, besides much else. He was outstanding as a preacher and a worker, and, *in spite of* his High Churchmanship (as one might say, for it was something of a novelty for the town), gained the respect and affection of all, and filled the church as it has never since been filled. He died in 1898, at the early age of 37.

The Advowson. The earliest information about the patronage in the diocesan records is for the year 1391, when the presentation to the living was in the hands of the Abbot and Convent of Wigmore (doubtless given them by the Mortimers). At the Reformation the patronage fell to the Crown. It was exercised by Queen Anne in 1702, but before 1720 had passed to the Earl of Oxford, in whose family it remained until about 1820. It has since changed hands five times, and is now with the Bishops of Hereford, the previous patron selling it in 1930 for £2,000, half of which sum was raised by members of the congregation.

Future generations will wonder why the congregation should have raised £1,000 merely to change the patron. For their benefit and that of others who may be concerned, it seems important that the explanation should be put on record here and now, while the matter is still within living memory. The subscribers wished, in fact, to ensure that the Church Council should in future have a voice in the appointment of new incumbents, and, in the belief that the Council would be so consulted, the money was subscribed. The Bishop, for his part, assured the Council (in writing) that he would consider it a moral obligation to consult their wishes in any nomination he made.

Acting doubtless in good faith, the Bishop obtained an Order in Council, which transferred the advowson to the Bishops of Hereford without condition. This probably happened after correspondence in the matter had ceased, so that the subscribers did not learn about the Order. Nor were they aware of it 10 years later, when the living next fell vacant, and they put their wishes before a new bishop. The latter had made his own choice, to which he got the Church Council to agree, in a firm but perfectly correct manner. . . . Be it remembered, however, that the congregation subscribed that not inconsiderable sum with a very definite object and understanding.

The previous patron probably lost on his deal. In fact, his price was considered generous. It is a pity that commercial language has to be used in such a connection. But what other language can be used when we read in the *Hereford Times* of 14th January, 1882, that the advowson was sold *by public auction* at the Mart, Tokenhouse Yard, for £5,000 ?

We do not know what price a rector rather previous to that time paid. This man was a bankrupt, with unsecured debts of over £11,000, paying his creditors 1s. 3d. in the £. He had bought the advowson of Presteigne and, the incumbency falling vacant shortly after the bankruptcy proceedings, he promptly inducted himself and promised his creditors £600 a year out of the proceeds. He paid this for 18 months, and then refused to pay any more. He was taken to court, and the Judge ordered him to resume his payments. He threatened a newspaper with a libel action for its comments on his behaviour, but it turned out that the newspaper had but repeated the Judge's remarks. On the whole, it would appear that a parish is not necessarily better off for being " a good living."

Or has Presteigne been particularly unfortunate ? Kilvert in his Diary (1874) has a story of yet another rector of Presteigne who was always "over head and ears in debt." Of this worthy, Kilvert writes : "He has every Sunday two Celebrations of the Holy Communion at which he always puts upon the plate his pocket knife by way of alms, saying that he has no change. After service he returns his knife to his pocket, but (it is stated) invariably forgets to *redeem* it."

Charities. Presteigne has an unusually long list of benefactors, from the time of the Elizabethan John Beddoes, who left land to pay for the ringing of the curfew (besides his Grammar School), to Thomas Pugh, who died in 1887 and whose charitable bequest is still distributed annually. A full list of all the benefactions up to the end of the 18th century will be found in Williams's History of Radnorshire. Doubtless some have passed into or through the hands of the Charity Commissioners. Several make provision for apprenticing poor children, and there are liberal gifts to the poor of coal, clothing and bread. John Matthews, gent., gave six bibles to six poor children " every year for ever." Giles Whitehall, of the Moor, Esq., gave the township in 1734 an engine for extinguishing fire and 12 leathern buckets.

Two of the benefactions had rather unusual origins. Thomas Cornewall, Baron, Lord of Stapleton and Lugharness, made his bequest from several sums of money of goods forfeited from felonies, murders, and other crimes. Judge Thomas Street gave £20, the amount of a fine paid by William Whitcomb, Sheriff, for his non-appearance at the Grand Assizes.

Altogether there were in the time of Williams 11 Charities providing annual benefits of some kind or other to the parish "for ever." The Charity Commissioners gave particulars of each one in their Report issued in 1838. There was a previous Parliamentary Return of 1786 which listed three others, but two of these had been lost before 1786, while the third seems to have disappeared between 1786 and 1838. It is clear that the same fate has overtaken some of the above 11—and there is none to say how or when. From the writer's experience of another Radnorshire parish, where three out of five old Charities had lapsed, lost Charities are not an unusual phenomenon, and usually the loss has been due to the negligence of the parishes themselves. Some of the Presteigne money bequests were invested in the name of the rector of the time. Who is to know what happened after his death? Future benefactors would do well to consult the Charity Commission (The Elms, Morecambe) before drawing up their bequests.

St. Ann's Well. This, situated at the far end of Brink Lane, was once famous as a holy well, though the name is almost forgotten now. The water was said to be an unfailing remedy for sore eyes, and the well was much resorted to for this purpose up to about 40 years ago.

XV

Felons and Vagabonds

It has been said of the 18th century, with some measure of truth, that there were only two castes in England, " one meekly submissive and liable to be hanged in batches at Tyburn for stealing a loaf of bread, the other strongly aristocratic, wealthy, insolent, and ignorant."*

When the 19th century opened over 200 offences were punishable by death. Property was sacred, of far more account than the lives of the poor, who were hanged if they stole anything of the value of 5s. or more. The alternative was transportation to " one of His Majesty's colonies."

As the seat of the county Great Sessions and the General Sessions, Presteigne saw much of the severity of the Law. The Judges came to the Great Sessions, which changed their name to the Assizes in 1830, when Wales came within the English circuit system. The County Magistrates presided at the General Sessions. The records of the Great Sessions and Assizes were removed to London in 1855, and none have been kept at Presteigne since that date. The records of the General Sessions are preserved at the Shire Hall from 1753. It is proposed in this chapter to give some account of the punishments shown in the latter, and to trace the gradual change to the milder standards of to-day.

Before dealing with the General Sessions, something should be said about the Great Sessions and the laws which they administered. It is not necessary to consult the records to know that the death sentence was passed as freely at Presteigne as elsewhere. There are plenty of references in the Rolls of the General Sessions to prisoners under sentence of death, and in the old files of the *Hereford Journal*, to confirm this, besides sundry entries in the church registers to the burial of executed felons. Hangings and transportations were the usual sentences up to 1820. In that year the Felony Repeal Acts were passed, which had the effect of reducing the number of offences punishable by death. Thefts from shops, warehouses, etc., for example, ceased to be capital offences unless the value of the stolen goods exceeded £15.

---

* A History of Music, by Stanford and Forsyth.

These Acts have a particular interest for Presteigne, since the man chiefly responsible for awakening the public conscience about capital punishment for thefts, etc., married a daughter of Francis Garbett, of Knill Court, and is buried in Knill church, within four miles of Presteigne. This was Sir Samuel Romilly, the Solicitor-General. His wife died in 1818 and, through grief at her death, he died by his own hand and was buried with her. He thus did not live to see the full fruit of his work. He managed in his lifetime to save pick-pockets from the gallows, but most of the enlightened reforms he tried to make were turned down by the aristocracy and bishops in the House of Lords.

The Shire Hall Rolls contain striking evidence of the immediate effect of the 1820 legislation. They include a " reprieve " of that year, signed by the king, for two men under sentence of death, one for horse stealing, the other for stealing goods valued at 5s. The " reprieve " ordained that the horse stealer should be transported for life, and the other offender for 7 years.

Horse stealing remained a capital offence until 1830, although the sentence was often commuted after 1820 to transportation for life. Sheep stealing was a capital offence until rather later than 1830, and up to that year executions for burglary or housebreaking were not uncommon.*

All executions were, of course, in public, and at Presteigne usually took place in front of the gaol. Public executions did not, in fact, cease until 1868, when they were abolished by the Capital Punishment Amendment Act.†

Perhaps sufficient has now been said about the severity of the Law in these earlier days to enable the reader to understand the mental outlook of the County Magistrates who passed the sentences recorded below. It is strange to us to-day to read that they, too, could inflict sentences of transportation, and could send prisoners to penal servitude. The magistrates for the old Borough of New Radnor had similar powers.

The earliest record of a sentence of transportation by the Presteigne magistrates is in 1825. Before that date the cases which came before them were chiefly petty thefts, assaults, and vagrancy, trivial affairs for the most part, though the punishments were by no means trivial. Even these, however, marked an advance in humanity compared with Elizabethan and Stuart times. We will

---

* In the three years 1828-30 there were 36 executions in England and Wales for burglary or housebreaking.

† For treason and other capital offences than murder, executions in public are still legal, though they invariably take place within the prison walls.

return to them later, after looking at a few of the heavier sentences, and seeing how those gradually became lighter, and more in accordance with present-day standards.

Here, then, are a few transportation sentences given by the magistrates, taken from the General Sessions records: In 1831, 14 years for a man who had sent a threatening letter to a solicitor; in 1837, life sentence for a man who had stolen a ram, valued at 10s.; in 1841, 10 years for attempted housebreaking; in 1844, 7 years for stealing a wether sheep, valued at 10s.; in 1845, 10 years for a man and woman who had stolen £15 " from the person "; in 1848, 7 years for stealing a ewe; in 1850, 7 years for stealing a horse.

In 1851 a burglar was sentenced to 7 years' transportation, and that is the last of such sentences recorded by the General Sessions.* A horse stealer in 1853 got only 12 months' hard labour, and in 1855 another got only three months, which is a remarkable change within the space of five years. Sentences for sheep stealing also became much milder; in 1862 a man who had stolen six wether sheep from one person and six from another got only 18 months' hard labour (nine for each offence).

As already mentioned, the magistrates could sentence prisoners to penal servitude. The first instance occurs in 1854, when a man previously convicted was sentenced to four years' penal servitude for stealing four hens and a chicken. The Court evidently had little sympathy for previous offenders, for, while two housebreakers got off with three years in 1858, in 1882 a woman previously convicted of larceny got five years' penal servitude and seven years' police supervision for stealing three aprons and three scarves from her employer. After that, it is good not to find any more mention of penal servitude in the Court's sentences. It marks, in fact, the last sentence of the Court which appears to be unduly severe, compared with present standards.

The magistrates have long ceased to have the power to try by themselves the more serious type of offences, such as horse stealing, burglary, etc. Under the Administration of Justice (Miscellaneous Provisions) Act, 1938, however, many indictments may now come before them which would ordinarily go to the Assizes, provided they have a legally qualified Chairman.

As regards the more trivial offences which came before the magistrates of the General Sessions up to about 1825, assaults were not a crime against property, and were generally let off lightly,

---

* Transportation as a punishment was abolished by an Act of 1857 (20 and 21 Vic. c.2.).

unless the person assaulted was a magistrate. A fine of 1s. was the usual penalty, but in 1802 a man who had assaulted a magistrate was fined 20s. and was to be imprisoned for three months, and not to be released until the fine was paid. Later, from about 1820, the fines were increased, and 20s. became a usual amount. But even in 1862 the Court thought two months' hard labour sufficient for one case of indecent assault, and one month for another, while sentencing a sheep stealer to 18 months.

Thefts and vagrancy were usually punished by a public whipping, to which a term of imprisonment was often added. Many whipping sentences are recorded. Invariably the culprits were stripped to the waist and flogged until the blood flowed. There is no record of a woman being whipped at Presteigne after 1788, but the public whipping of women (who were stripped like the men) was not stopped until 1817. A further Act of 1820* prohibited the private whipping of women (to which privileged spectators used to be admitted, such were the times). The last instance of a man being publicly whipped at Presteigne was in 1828.

Here are some whipping sentences, taken from the Presteigne records: 16 July, 1783.—A woman found guilty of larceny: " The sentence of the Court is that Anne W——, the prisoner, on Saturday seven-night between the hours of twelve and one o'clock at noon be stripped from the wast (so spelt) upwards and publickly whipped by the gaoler at the Market House in Presteigne for a quarter of an hour on the bare back till the blood comes and be confined till the sentence is executed and then discharged upon payment of fees."

8 October, 1788. A woman who had stolen goods worth 10d.; " To be whipped on her bare back at the Cart's Tail from the Gaol door by the Market House to the Castle and back to the Gaol on Saturday next between the hours of twelve and one o'clock."

12 January, 1803.—Man convicted of larceny in milking cows: " To be imprisoned until Saturday, 12 February, and at 12 to be tied to a cart to be drawn by one horse and whipped on the naked back by the gaoler or his deputy through the publick street from the Gaol door to the Town Hall in Presteigne and back again to the Gaol door and then discharged."

The whipping invariably took place on Saturday, which was market day. The gaol in those days was on the present site of the Shire Hall in Broad Street, and the Town Hall and Market House were at the top of Broad Street.

---

* The two Acts were 57 Geo. III c. 75, and 1 Geo. IV c. 57.

Prisoners from other towns were sent to their native places for the whipping. Thus in 1787 a man was to be whipped round Knighton; in 1801 a man (for milking cows) was to receive 24 lashes at Painscastle; and in 1803 a man (for larceny) was to receive " not less than 100 lashes " at Llowes. The usual provision " until his back be bloody " was made in the last-mentioned case, but it seems rather superfluous.

In 1807, a man, for stealing a shirt, besides being whipped from the gaol door to the market place and back, was sentenced to three months' solitary confinement. There are a number of instances in the records of this latter cruel form of punishment, from 1798 onwards, though later such a long term as three months was prohibited. The last case was in 1870, when a man received 12 months' hard labour for housebreaking, the first two and the last two weeks to be in solitary confinement.

Vagrants had a bad reception if it could be proved against them that they were " rogues and vagabonds," more especially that they were " incorrigible rogues." They got a public whipping and up to 6 months' hard labour as well. According to a Consolidating Act of 1822,* " incorrigible rogues " might get up to a year's hard labour for the first offence, and up to two years for the second offence. The General Sessions do not appear to have dealt with these offenders after 1826, and presumably left them to the Petty Sessions.

It must have been a ticklish matter to decide whether or not a person was a rogue and a vagabond. A man who was so called by a Petty Sessions verdict in 1858, and who was sentenced to three months' imprisonment, appealed to the General Sessions, where it was decided that he was not a rogue and a vagabond and that the magistrates responsible should pay £9 16s. 2d. costs.

To conclude the chapter on a lighter note, we might quote from two documents among the Rolls for 1761 and 1763. The first, of 1761, reads:

" Be it remembered that on the sixth day of February in the second year of His Majesty's reign Henry Williams was convicted before me one of His Majesty's Justices of the Peace of the said County for swearing six prophane oaths . . ."

A similar indictment follows for Stephen Mynton, who swore 33 " prophane oaths."

Unfortunately there is no record to show what the General Sessions magistrates did to soothe the outraged feelings of their

---

* 3 Geo. IV c. 40.

brother-magistrate.   Nor do we know what they did about the 1763 petition of John Jenkins of Clyro, who lost most of his possessions through " a terrible fire " and " therefore Humbley Prays the permission of this Honble. Court to Travel through the County of Radnor for the space of six months to aske the Charity and Mulifisence of all well disposed persons in some measure to redress your Petitioner's Loss."   We will hope that John Jenkins was granted his petition and could proceed on his way without fear of being seized upon as a rogue and a vagabond.

Parish Church.

A Study in Contours

Clock on Assembly Rooms.

(To face page 96).

St. David's Street   *Bull Hotel.*

West Wall   *Old woollen factory at end.*

(To face page 97).

XVI

Inside the Gaol

Since Presteigne derived so much of its early importance from being the seat of the County Sessions and Gaol, no excuse seems to be required for devoting a further chapter to this subject. Enough has been said to give an idea of the Sessional proceedings. This chapter will deal more particularly with the gaol and its management.

First, as regards the old building on the Shire Hall site, which was used until the new one was opened in 1822, on the present site of the County School by the Clatter Brook. There are no pictures of this early gaol, and we do not know what it was like or when it was built. It was kept by a gaoler and his wife, with only occasional help from outside, and, judging from other gaols of the period, was probably small, with little light or ventilation, a place in which prisoners were herded like cattle, and the more refractory put in cells of indescribable filth and gloom.

In the language of Lord Cockburn, the gaols were " dirty, foetid, cruel hells of torture and demoralisation." Here is a description in *The Times* of 13 January, 1844, of a prison in Birmingham, in which 23 debtors were placed: " a confined, ill-ventilated hole, the area of which was 6 feet by 9, underground, and made out of the cellar of an old house, and from which the stench was intolerable."

There is a letter among the Presteigne Sessional Rolls addressed to the magistrates from a new gaoler appointed in 1815, in which the latter asks for more furniture, etc., and points out that the gaol only possessed the following: 14 very bad blankets, one old dresser with two drawers, five three-legged stools, four small benches, and one small bucket. Blankets were first served to the prisoners in 1810. Previously they had only straw for their bedding: " straw for the prisoners " is a regular item in the early accounts, and it was used to supplement the blankets after 1810.

Food for the prisoners consisted of 1 lb. of bread daily, which allowance was increased to 1½ lb. in 1809. No doubt those who could afford to pay got extra rations. Until 1811, when the gaoler's salary was increased to £30 per annum, he received only

£20, and he relied on " garnish " from the prisoners for supplying them with extras at his own price. In most gaols there was a " tap," from which the gaoler supplied liquor to the prisoners, at considerable profit to himself. At Presteigne this was closed in 1785, at the gaoler's own request, and an allowance of £13 per annum (later reduced to £8) added to his income.

From some of the earlier Rolls it seems that prisoners were not even guaranteed a free bread allowance. There are several orders of magistrates to the gaoler like the following of 1763: " Information hath been made unto me that Thomas Evans of the Parish of Llanyear, a Poor Prisoner now in ye County Gaol, is in great Distress. You are heare by ordered to give him the usual allowance of the County Bread untill further orders." There were also two orders in 1797 that " no bread be allowed in future " to certain debtors in the gaol.

The number of prisoners appears to have averaged about 12. No attempt was made to segregate males and females. Even in the new and far better gaol of 1822 it was left to a prison inspector of 1837 to suggest " the erection of a few cells for the reception of females, wholly removed and distinct from those of males." Several escapes are recorded from the old gaol, but the gaoler did his best to prevent these by keeping the most active of the prisoners in irons. Those under sentence of death were invariably kept in irons during the two days which elapsed between their sentence and execution.

There are many bills for " ironing " the prisoners among the Rolls, usually at 2s. a time. In 1827 4s. was paid for " double-ironing " a prisoner. Even those in gaol " on suspicion " appear to have been ironed. In 1762 4s. was charged for putting bolts, shackles and rivets on John Cadwallader " that was in on suspicion." In 1755 1s. was charged for ironing " the Irishman " and 2s. 6d. for " putting two pare of irons and rivets on Pugh of Evenjob," against 2s. for various other " fellons."

Ironing itself did not always prevent escapes. An advertisement appeared in the Police Gazette of 9 September, 1820, offering 20 guineas reward for the apprehension of a man under sentence of death who escaped from H.M. Gaol at Presteigne on 24 August, and who " had on only his shirt and was doubly ironed."

The gaoler was allowed to employ assistants on special occasions. A rather gruesome entry occurs in the minutes of 1822: " That the Treasurer do pay to Thomas Meredith the sum of one pound for acting as turnkey two days and two nights sitting up with a convict whilst the Gaoler was absent in search of an Executioner."

We have already referred to the Felony Repeal Acts of 1820, which removed the death penalty for various offences. No less important were further Acts passed in 1823 and 1824, which aimed at improving conditions in gaols. One has but to read them to realise how appalling these conditions were, to make necessary such elementary and reasonable reforms. They included provisions that the sexes should be segregated and female prisoners put under the care of a matron; that prison " taps " should everywhere be abolished, and no liquor served to the prisoners; that food should be provided for prisoners committed for trial, even though they could not work for it; and that no prisoner should be put on the treadmill before conviction. For some years after 1824 the prisoners received no part of their earnings at hard labour, which were given to the County funds.

The first mention of the appointment of magistrates to visit the gaol occurs in 1815. They were " to be at liberty to order supplies of soap, coal, and other necessaries for the criminals," and also repairs up to £50. Had there been visiting magistrates before that date they would, we will suppose, have discovered the poor fellow under sentence of seven years' transportation who was actually left in the gaol for that space of time. A belated petition for mercy on his behalf was made by the Court in 1785.

There was, of course, a gaol chaplain. According to an entry of 1774, he received two guineas for attending felons at their execution, and 7s. 6d. for printing their confessions. He was given a salary of £15 per annum in 1814, and a little later 25 guineas, in return for which he attended condemned prisoners, and did duty at the gaol every Sunday, on the Great Festivals, and the whole of Passion Week. Sometimes the rector of Presteigne acted as chaplain, and it was one such to whom the Clerk of the Peace was ordered in 1818 "to write respectfully that the two prisoners in the gaol under sentence of death are reported to the Court not to have been visited by him." The gaol was almost opposite his house.

If we do not know much about the old gaol, we know a good deal about the later one on the County School site, because we have the full report of a Committee appointed to inspect the gaol. It was divided into three departments, (1) The Felons, (2) The Debtors,* and (3) The House of Correction. In both (1) and (3) there were 10 cells, and the debtors had 12 " rooms." No heat was provided and no artificial light, but each department had a day room where, subject to good behaviour, the prisoners were

---

* Imprisonment for debt was abolished by the Debtors' Act of 1869. There were usually five or six debtors in the Presteigne gaol.

allowed to sit from 7 a.m. to 7 p.m. from 1 June to 30 September, and from 8 a.m. to 7 p.m. for the rest of the year, when a fire was provided and also a candle.

Each day room had a table and a bench. There was a large bathing tub in the wash-house where all prisoners washed, their own furniture only running to an iron bedstead with clothes, a wooden stool and a pewter utensil,—debtors having also a table, and a chair instead of a stool. An old resident, who visited the gaol after it was closed, remembers seeing this cheering inscription on the walls of the felons' day room : " Remember, your sins will find you out."

The gaoler still had no regular staff. He was to visit each prisoner at least once a day, and the Committee thought, as he had the care of female prisoners, it was important he should be a married man, and that his wife should be responsible for super-intending the female prisoners. He was permitted a servant maid, who was to be paid not more than £6 per annum. He himself was to have £65 per annum, and to act as Keeper of the House of Correction, as well as gaoler. " Garnish " in any shape or form was forbidden.

Prisoners were not to be put in irons without the knowledge and consent of a magistrate. The gaol had a " drop " for execu-tions. It also had a corn mill and a bakehouse, besides a chapel, two sick rooms and four airing yards. Prisoners on hard labour were put to work at the crank mill or stone breaking.

The dietary of the prisoners remained at 1½ lb. of bread a day until 1828, when it was changed to 1 lb. of bread and 2 lb. of potatoes each day, with meat once a week, soup twice, and herrings twice. Gruel was added some 10 years later, but no substantial change was made until 1850* when, by order of the Secretary of State, a new dietary was established, in which the quantities of food were graded according to the term of imprisonment and by sex; bread, potatoes and gruel were still the staple items, but prisoners in for longer terms or on hard labour got meat or soup in addition on certain days. Cheese was added in 1870 for the latter classes on Sundays, their dinner that day consisting of bread and cheese only. Such items as tea, butter, sugar and milk were not included in the dietary even in 1870.

By 1847 the gaoler had become known as the Governor of the Gaol and House of Correction, but he still had no staff beyond his wife, who had acquired the title of Matron; his salary was fixed at £70. Even in 1865 there was only one turnkey.†

---

* Except for debtors, whose dietary was slightly improved in 1846.
† The term warder, instead of turnkey, first occurs in the records in 1873.

The Prisons Act of the same year required that there should be 3 male turnkeys and one female turnkey, and that the gaol should be enlarged. The average number of prisoners at that time was only 13, but a proposal to transfer the prisoners to Hereford apparently hurt the pride of the magistrates, who went to the expense of making the necessary alterations. They appear to have done it as cheaply as possible; the " general servant " of the governor was to act as female turnkey, at an annual salary of not more than £12.

To conclude the history of the gaol. It ceased to be used as a gaol in 1878, under the Prisons Act of 1877. By that time the average daily number of prisoners was less than 6. The prisoners were moved to Hereford, and part of the gaol was used as a lock-up until 1886, when the building was finally vacated.

Some readers may wonder what the House of Correction was. It was primarily a place of detention for " rogues, vagabonds and sturdy beggars." A statute of Queen Elizabeth directed that each county should possess one. Later it served for the imprisonment of all poor people who refused to employ themselves on appointed work, and for those who set the parish constable at defiance. At Presteigne part of the gaol was used for the purpose until 1793, when an adjoining building was made the House of Correction. The County Magistrates sometimes sent offenders there " for close and solitary confinement." Mention of the House of Correction occurs in the minutes up to 1879.

A picturesque feature at the Shire Hall proceedings were the 12 javelin men, who attended the Sheriff, kept order at the Sessions, and at executions. Each Sheriff provided a new set of javelins, and there are still parts of two sets in private houses at Presteigne.* In most counties the javelin men disappeared about 1860, but at Presteigne they were retained until 1870, when their duties were taken over by the police.

The Shire Hall records give a good deal of information about the police force, which was first created in Radnorshire in 1857, and its subsequent development, but the story belongs to the county rather than to Presteigne itself. It might be mentioned that the original force consisted of a Chief Constable, who acted for Herefordshire and Radnorshire, two superintendents, two sergeants, and 10 constables, the latter receiving 21s. first class and 19s. second class. Four additional constables were temporarily appointed in 1863, when the railway at Rhayader was under construction. The County got its own Chief Constable in 1867: he resided at Penybont.

---

* In one case the " javelins," of later date than the others, are actually halberds, evidently made for ornament rather than for use.

XVII

Tales and Travels

This is not a Guide Book in the ordinary sense, but a book about Presteigne would seem incomplete without some reference to its setting and the places of most interest which are near. The hills which surround it are split up into many valleys, which make Presteigne and its green belt their meeting place, and in whatever direction a person leaves the town he encounters beauty on every side, sufficiently diverse to make each walk in turn a fresh delight. To add to his pleasure, everywhere there is a profusion of wild flowers,—masses of snowdrops, daffodils and primroses in the spring, and in summer-time bluebells, foxgloves, and honeysuckle.

Connected with some of the places there are stories or associations, which will be mentioned hereafter. Before proceeding, however, there is a story about Presteigne which should be told. This concerns a famous duel which arose out of a quarrel at the Oak Inn in Broad Street and resulted in the death of one of the combatants. The quarrel is said to have occurred at a cockfight,* though, as both combatants had their swords, some suppose it was an old-standing affair, and that the duel had been planned beforehand.

The exact date of the occurrence is not known, but it appears to have been in the early part of the 18th century. The antagonists were James Baskerville, of Aberedw, and the Squire of Boultibrooke, believed to have been a Colonel Lloyd. The latter was killed, and it was said that '' the family of Baskerville from the time of this unfortunate event never prospered.'' The duel took place in the upper storey of an outbuilding behind 9, Broad Street, and the wooden casement is still shown which was opened to provide light for the combatants.

Old people in the town remember hearing of a duel fought with pistols on Burfa Bank '' long ago,'' but no one now knows when or by whom. Such stories, when they persist, have usually a foundation of truth. This one appears to be supported by the

---

* The Oak was famed for its cockfighting, which long remained a favourite '' sport,'' though made illegal by the Cruelty to Animals Act, 1849.

fact that a pistol was found about 70 years ago near the flat piece of ground where the duel is supposed to have been fought, and is now in the possession of an old resident, who has shown it to the writer. It appears to be an 18th century flint-lock, complete with ramrod; length 15½ inches.

The last duel known to the writer to have been fought in Wales took place at Tenby in 1839, when one of the combatants was killed. A Worcester solicitor, challenged to a duel two years earlier, got his opponent bound over in £400 to keep the peace.

Most of the famous people connected with Presteigne have already been mentioned. Apart from Bishop Martin, it does not appear to have produced anyone of outstanding importance, unless we except Richard Lucas, D.D. The latter was born at Presteigne in 1648, and after leaving Oxford University, became a famous preacher in London and a prebend of Westminster. He lost his sight in middle life, but acquired fame with his devotional writings, especially his '' Enquiry after Happiness,'' which went through many editions and was a favourite work with John Wesley, who, we read, '' retained the cordiality of the attachment he conceived for Lucas to the last year of his life.'' Dr. Lucas died in 1715.

Stapleton Castle is barely a mile from Presteigne, over the Lugg bridge. It is a picturesque ruin and in pretty surroundings. Something of its history has already been told in the chapter, *Peace and War*. It stands on the site of an ancient motte and bailey, which date from at least Norman times. The old castle was '' slighted '' in 1645, and the present ruins are probably a re-building of about that time; the brick arches on the east front are of rather later date. A family of the name of Galliers was the last to occupy the castle, which was finally vacated about 100 years ago.

The castle was in the hands of the Cornewall family for centuries. The first Cornewall to live there was a great-nephew of Henry III, and, as we have seen, a later Cornewall of Stapleton married a sister of Henry IV. Originally the castle belonged to the de Say family of Richard's Castle (*see p.* 20). The lord of this castle married a sister of the Fair Rosamund, the mistress of Henry II, who, it is possible, therefore visited Stapleton, her own brother having estates in the neighbourhood. We know that Henry II passed through Presteigne in 1163. Those romantically inclined may like to imagine a meeting between the two on that occasion. At any rate, it is a possibility.

Stapleton has its ghost. Apparently a servant of the castle (it may have been in the 17th century) fell in love with his mistress, drowned her husband in the Lugg, and, failing to get his love returned, murdered the lady. Her phantom is said to haunt the castle and lanes round about. She is known as Lady Bluefoot, and there is an old rhyme about her which Presteigne children were taught. It ran:—

> Lady Bluefoot, all in black,
> Silver buttons down her back.
> Harrigoshee! Harrigoshee!
> Lock the cupboard and take the key.

It is related that an infant child of the murdered couple was smuggled abroad, and returned as a young man to wreak dire vengeance on the murderer.

Another version of the murder makes the poor lady's husband the murderer. He had, it is said, wrongfully accused her of infidelity. She affirmed her innocence and foretold that, to prove it, after her death white violets would evermore grow around the castle at Christmas time. Whether or not this version of the story be true, white violets may usually be seen near Stapleton castle at Christmas.

Most of the cottages around the castle are of the 17th century, and one (Carter's Croft) was built in the 13th or 14th century; it has crutch trusses and a continuous original roof.

Those, by the way, who are interested in medieval domestic architecture will find a number of specimens among the farms and cottages in the neighbourhood of Presteigne. Parts of Highland Farm, south of Wapley Hill, for instance, and of Combe Farm, north of Wapley Hill, the Little Rodd, Old Wegnall Farm, Lower Court at Kinsham, Mynachty, near Pilleth, Court Farm at Walton, and a number of houses at Pembridge and Lyonshall. Rather further afield, Chapel Farm, a mile or so on the Lingen side of Wigmore, is a very good example of a 15th century building.

There are many examples of 16th and 17th century buildings within two or three miles of Presteigne, in addition to those in the town. They include the building behind the Cat and Fiddle, Broad Heath, Court House, Byton, Staunton Old Hall, Nash Farm, Little Brampton Farm, Old Impton Farm at Norton, and Burfa Farm at the foot of Burfa Hill. Most of the houses around Willey have 16th or 17th century features (e.g., Old Hall and Willey Lodge). Willey Court, now a ruin, probably had a much earlier origin; local tradition says it was a monastic foundation. At Old Hall (anciently Netherall) lived Hugh Wylley, Groom of the Chamber to Henry VIII.

The Rodd, in the occupation of Lord Rennell of Rodd, is an unusually fine specimen of a Jacobean manor house; it was completed in 1629 and has much good contemporary work inside, including panelling, mantelpieces, and moulded ceilings. There is a tradition that the plague at Presteigne held up work on the house, and that this and the subsequent exaction of Ship Money somewhat cramped the style of the original owners of Rodd, who were ancestors of Lord Rennell. (The family name of Rodd comes from this manor and others in Cornwall and Devonshire.)

A person famous in local history lived at Nash Court, which, like the Rodd, is within the ecclesiastical parish of Presteigne. This was Elin Gethin—in English, Ellen the Terrible—wife of Thomas Vaughan, of Hergest. To avenge her brother, who was killed in a family quarrel at Llwynwent, near Llanbister, she disguised herself as a man and went to an archery meeting at Llanddewi Ystradenny, where the murderer was one of the competitors. When it came to her turn to shoot, she directed her arrow at the murderer and killed him on the spot.

After her husband had been killed fighting on the Yorkist side at the battle of Banbury in 1469, she retired to a property of hers at Nash, and in 1474 obtained an Indulgence for those who would pray for the soul of her husband. We can imagine this being proclaimed in Presteigne church, which Ellen Vaughan probably attended. She shares the altar tomb of her husband in Kington church, where the beautiful effigies of both may still be seen. Their home, Hergest Croft (from which the Red Book of Hergest gets its name) is now a farmhouse; it is a mile or so the other side of Kington, and preserves parts of the original building.

Boultibrooke, with its beautiful grounds and gardens, dates back at least to Henry VIII's reign, though little of the present house is of earlier date than the 18th century. Nantygroes, between Whitton and Pilleth, is another house with a long history. It was once the home of the ancestors of Dr. John Dee, the alchemist, of Queen Elizabeth's time. Though much modernised, it preserves a few old features.

Kinsham Court and Eywood are both fine 18th century hou es, within four miles or so of Presteigne, and in surroundings of exceptional beauty. The former is now the home of Sir John Arkwright, the writer of the well-known Hymn of Sacrifice, '' O valiant hearts who to your glory came.'' Both houses once belonged to the Harleys, Earls of Oxford, Eywood being built by a brother of the first Earl, the famous Robert Harley. Kinsham Court was also the home of Florence Nightingale when a child. It was during the Harley occupation that Lord Byron was a visitor to both houses. He dedicated his poem '' Childe Harold '' to Lady Charlotte Harley, daughter of the fifth Earl, and is said to have written some of the poem at Kinsham. As the Kinsham family was frequently in Presteigne, it seems safe to assume that Byron also came here.

It is possible that another great poet knew Presteigne. Wordsworth's connection with Brinsop in Herefordshire is well known. Not so well known is the fact that he and his wife used to visit an aunt (Miss Hutchinson) of the latter, who lived in a house near the Crooked Well, Kington. The signatures of the poet's wife and son appear on the deeds of the house, and there is a Scotch fir in front of the house which was planted by Wordsworth himself. He is known to have travelled round the district and to have attended services at a Friends' Meeting House at Walton (pulled down four or five years ago). At Kington, by the way, the great Mrs. Siddons made her first stage appearance—in a barn behind the Talbot Hotel.

Frances Ridley Havergal, the hymn writer, was a frequent visitor to Presteigne. She used to stay at Highland Farm, and went about the district on a donkey. There is a large yew tree by the Warren on top of Wapley Hill under which she is said to have composed some of her hymns.

Before writing briefly of " travels " around Presteigne, a word of advice might be given about maps. For most purposes the Ordnance Survey One Inch to One Mile Sheet No. 80 will serve. This takes in the whole of Radnor Forest, but does not extend to Knighton, or indeed more than four miles *north* of Presteigne. Beyond this limit Sheet No. 70 would be required.

For walkers who wish to leave the roads and use trackways and field paths—which abound in this countryside—the Ordnance Survey Six Inch to One Mile maps are strongly recommended. They are the key to many untrodden ways and hidden splendours, and unfold the country as no guide book can do. They can be had on application to Messrs. E. Stanford, Ltd., 12-14, Long Acre, London, W.C.2, and cost 2s. each.* The following collection of ten sheets covers all the country within a radius of four or five miles of Presteigne: Radnorshire XXV N.W., N.E., S.E., S.W.; and XVIII, N.W., N.E., S.E., S.W.; Herefordshire VI, S.W.; and XI, N.W. If Knighton is required, add Radnorshire XI S.W.; if Kington is required, add Herefordshire XVII N.E.

Presteigne is a good centre from which to explore Offa's Dyke. Armed with these maps, the explorer will need no directions for finding the Dyke and following it for the whole of its course through Radnorshire, starting from Knighton, and finishing on Rushock Hill, above Knill. The total distance is some 12 or 13 miles, for most of which the Dyke is plainly visible—a high bank,

---

* During war-time applications have to be accompanied by a licence obtainable from a Chief of Police, who would wish to know the purpose for which the maps are required.

with a ditch on its western side. If this distance is too long, then the journey might be broken at Burfa (nine miles), and the return to Presteigne made by road—another five miles, which is about the distance from Rushock.

The Dyke was made by local labour working to the plans of the military engineers of King Offa of Mercia (who reigned 757-796). It marked the boundary between Mercia and Wales, and was made for this purpose rather than defence. Any Welshman found on the English side was liable to severe penalties. The boundary line stretched a distance of 149 miles, from the Dee to the Severn. The total length of constructed earthwork was 80 miles. One of the objects of the builders was to give the Dyke as wide a view as possible, particularly on the Welsh side. How well they succeeded in their design in Radnorshire let the walker himself determine—for surely there is not a lovelier walk in Britain.

Those who wish to see a short stretch of the Dyke at its best, without walking the whole distance, should go to Yew Tree Farm, about half a mile beyond Discoed, turn left and walk the Dyke a mile or so to the road by Pen Offa Farm. The return to Presteigne can be made along the ancient track leading to Cold Oak and the Slough. Just beyond Pen Offa is Castle Ring, a small British camp with its banks well preserved, probably constructed after the Romans left Britain. Several early stone spinning whorls have been found around Pen Offa Farm.

The British camp on Wapley Hill (already mentioned as associated with Caractacus) has an area of 25 acres, and five lines of ramparts on one side and four on another. This and the camp on Burfa Hill, which is almost as large, are two of the finest pre-Roman camps on the Welsh border. One authority says that 15 counties can be seen from the top of Wapley, another says eight. The view is certainly remarkable, taking in the Carmarthen Vans, the Brecon Beacons, the Sugar Loaf, the Malverns, Clees, Longmynd, and some of the Montgomery hills, besides Radnor Forest. It is less than three miles from Presteigne, approached by Highland Farm. Cole's Hill, the peaked hill to the north-east of the town (1,097 feet), also makes a pleasant excursion by way of Letchmoor Lane, though it has no camp. Cole is the old English word for magician. The late Alfred Watkins, of the Woolhope Club, thought that the hill was an important sighting point of the prehistoric track makers—the ley makers—whom he surmised ranked as magicians. Hence, the Magician's Hill. Hell Peak nearby and the hill above the Frith Wood are rich in fossils.

The visitor to Presteigne may be left to find other beauty spots for himself. On every side there are little Arcadies offering fresh delights. Hills and valleys, woods and streams, unspoiled in their seclusion, are everywhere for the asking. Follow the Lugg below Kinsham; and the old road to Evenjobb by the Slough and Cold Oak, for two different types of scenery, each of great attraction. Striking off to the left from the Lugg, the walker will find the 13th century ruins of Limebrook Nunnery in a romantic situation, and continuing to Lingen (whose church has two 14th century bells and a sanctus), a very beautiful walk of 12 or 13 miles may be rounded off by returning to Presteigne through Stapleton. A delightful day may also be spent in the neighbourhood of Willey, Harley's Mountain, and beyond.

Norton, Willey, Wapley, Knill, Cold Oak, Discoed are all focal points of beauty. There is a fine view from near the monument on the highest part of the road to Knighton, and a charming walk back to Norton through woods. The walk by Stocking Farm and Stonewall Hill to Knighton, along another old road, lifts the walker among curlews and plovers, and is memorable for its wide views. The bus might be used for the outward or return journey of these two walks. There is one bus journey in particular which is strongly to be recommended—from Knighton to Newtown, 20 miles of typical mid-Wales scenery, the road rising to over 1,500 feet.*

Knighton is rather outside our radius, but it is easily reached by bus, and is worth a visit for its setting among hills. Few towns can have more beautiful approaches, and the two-mile walk to Stowe (whose church has an ancient roof, some good modern glass, and two bells of 1200), in one direction, and about the same distance out and back along the Penybont road in the opposite direction, will well repay the traveller for his exertions.

Radnor Forest, too, is hardly within easy walking distance of Presteigne, but every visitor to Presteigne will want to see something of its wonderful moorland scenery. Cyclists can readily get to it by way of New Radnor or Bleddfa. For pedestrians, perhaps the best approach is from Cascob, or by Beggar's Bush and the old track which leaves the New Radnor road a short distance beyond the Bush. The Forest can, however, be reached by another method; this is to take the bus to Knighton and then the train to Dolau, which is less than a mile from Llanfihangel Rhydithon, at the foot of the Forest. From there a walk of say three miles along the ancient trackway which crosses the Forest will give as good an impression of the Forest as can be got anywhere. The Forest and surrounding hills were infested with wolves until Tudor times; it is on record that the last wolf was killed at that period near Cregrina.

---

* Ring up Knighton 3 for days and times of buses.

If there is a homesick Englishman who would like to see some typical English scenery for a change, let him walk or cycle the five or six miles to Staunton-on-Arrow, approaching it by the narrow road which leaves the Kington road. He will see, at the right season, masses of willow herb on the way, a pretty English hamlet, and, from the castle mound, a view which will bring to mind the Weald of Kent or Sussex. Another delightful excursion of about the same distance is *via* Titley Junction to Lyonshall, where, besides old houses, can be seen some ruins of the castle, standing within a moat, and an impressive piece of Offa's Dyke.

Students of church architecture will not need to be reminded of the interest to be found in Herefordshire churches, so many of them rich in Norman work. Three of the best near Presteigne can be reached by train. They are Pembridge, Eardisland and Kingsland, which can all be seen in a day by leaving the train at Pembridge, and walking the six miles through Eardisland to Kingsland, from where the return journey can be made to Presteigne. The three villages are among the prettiest in the county, with many black and white houses. Kingsland is near the site of the battle of Mortimer's Cross. Byton church, nearer at hand, is modern, but has a Saxon font with Norman decoration, and a Norman tympanum.

Shobdon church, seven miles from Presteigne, should be seen if possible for the beauty of its surroundings, and its unique interior, which, finished in white enamel and light blue upholstery, is much as it was left by its nobleman builder of the 18th century. He gave it an Oriental mosque-like touch, in honour, it is said, of an Indian princess who was visiting the family. The church preserves a fine Norman font, but the rest of the Norman building, which rivalled Kilpeck for its sculptures, was pulled down by the said nobleman in 1753, and the choicest pieces of it were re-erected in his grounds, to improve the landscape. They may still be seen with their rare carvings, but these will soon become obliterated by constant exposure to the weather. To-day we stand aghast at the effrontery which could so destroy a priceless gem of architecture.

Radnorshire churches are usually small, many of them have been " restored " beyond recognition or rebuilt, the old work is mostly not later than the 14th or 15th century, and there are very few Norman remains. The county was famed for its woodwork in the 15th century, and a number of the churches have preserved screens of this period; those at Old Radnor and Llananno (near Llanbister) are among the best in Britain.

Old Radnor church (seven miles) is one of the most interesting churches in Wales, and besides its magnificent screen, has a wooden organ case of 1500, a beautiful old roof with good carvings, old tiles and glass, and a Celtic font of the 5th or 6th century. Knill church is just outside the county: it has a pretty situation, and preserves a Norman font and window, and a 14th century church-yard cross. Knill Court, the home for centuries of the Knill and Walsham families, was burnt down in 1943.

Typical small Radnorshire churches can be seen at Cascob (six miles) and Pilleth (five miles). Cascob is mainly 13th century and has an old screen and roof: it stands amid beautiful surroundings. Pilleth, near where the battle was fought in 1402, is 14th century, and has an ancient dug-out chest. Pilleth Court dates from the time of Henry VIII, and there is a fine Norman motte and bailey by the river. Further afield, other Radnorshire churches of out-standing interest are Glascwm (which St. David himself is said to have founded); Rhulen nearby, surely one of the most primitive in Wales and in the loveliest surroundings; Llanbister, another Celtic foundation and largely 13th century; and Disserth, with its 17th century interior almost intact.

XVIII

Odds and Ends

Someone who had kindly supplied much useful information about old Presteigne asked the writer whether he was mentioning Sir Archibald in this book, whereupon the writer had to confess that he had not heard of that gentleman. It turned out that Sir Archibald was a famous pedigree Hereford bull who flourished in the 1880's and belonged to Mr. Ben Rogers, a well-known breeder, who lived at the Rodd Farm. This gave the writer the idea that some names of the fairly recent past ought to be included in this book—but of people, and not bulls—that is, names of people who, though they do not figure in history, contributed to the administrative or civic life of Presteigne in their day. Many of the names, no doubt, were household words in the Presteigne that once was. Some present names are included, since they, too, may be names of the past, when another book comes to be written about Presteigne.

Then there is the story of Cecil Parsons and the Radnorshire Cottagers, which is buried in the newspaper files of over 100 years ago, and might well now be rescued from oblivion. There are other Presteigne stories which appear worth the telling before they, too, are forgotten. With such a variety of subjects, it is proposed to call this chapter Odds and Ends, and deal with each subject under its own heading, starting with the stories.

The End of an Evil Spirit.

In the 1911 Transactions of the Honourable Society of Cymmrodorion there appeared an informative article by the Rev. D. Edmondes Owen, entitled " Pre-Reformation Survivals in Radnorshire ". The writer showed how some of the old church observances lingered in Radnorshire up to the 18th and early 19th centuries, and traced back to Pre-Reformation teaching and practice many of the customs and beliefs still current in the county. In the light of that article the following story need cause little surprise.

It concerns the Vaughans of Hergest, to whom reference has already been made (*see* page 105). The story of the *Black Dog* of Hergest and his ghostly appearances has been told by Conan Doyle, though he lays its scene in Devonshire and calls it "The Hound of the Baskervilles" (who were related to the Vaughans). That story, however, hardly concerns Presteigne, beyond the fact that the dog is said to roam the hills round there, and the writer knows people who aver that they have seen it. This story concerns the *Black Vaughan* of Hergest, who was killed by the said hound somewhere about the end of the 17th century.

Never did ghost perform a more meritorious service, for this Vaughan appears to have collected to himself most of the iniquities of mankind, and to have been feared and hated accordingly. Unfortunately for the neighbourhood, his spirit stayed behind and caused no end of trouble, particularly to farmers on their way home from Kington market, mounting their ponies and stealing their purchases from under their frightened eyes. In fact, it looked as if the Black Vaughan had cheated Satan, as he had said he would, when he caused his face to be carved over the kitchen mantelpiece and a pair of cherubic wings attached thereto (they may still be seen), boasting that when Satan saw the wings he would never claim the spirit of one so obviously bound for Heaven. The angels, of course, were less easily deceived, and had their own reasons for not taking the soul of the departed.

In such circumstances the only course to get rid of the nuisance was clearly to resort to human agency, and have the spirit exorcised "by bell, book and candle." Presteigne church was chosen for the scene of the encounter, and thither came all the parsons of the district to perform their task. Assembled in the church they formed a circle in which the evil spirit was summoned to appear. What they did afterwards and what shape the spirit assumed we are not told. Perhaps they reduced the spirit to the form of a bluebottle, as did Parson Jones with the scoundrelly spirit he subdued in Disserth church, in the story related by Edmondes Owen. Reduce it they did, and so successfully that they were able to enclose it in a snuff box. This box was then taken to Hergest and put in the pond there and covered with a huge stone—which anyone may see to-day, for it remains above the water.

To make doubly sure that the spirit should not reappear, the parsons directed that the stone should not be moved for 200 years. When that period expired, during the last Great War, the owner of Hergest decided to take the risk of moving the stone and opening the box. But, in spite of a careful search, *no box was to be found.* We are left wondering whether the Black Vaughan was too clever for his adversaries, or whether someone else was in the end too clever for the Black Vaughan, and took him, box and all. Or were the parsons more clever than we suppose?

NOTE.—It should perhaps be added that the story of the exorcism in Presteigne Church is founded on what appears to be a well-established local tradition. It was recorded in writing by an old lady (Miss Fawcett) who died at Kington many years ago, and who heard it from several old people in whose families the tradition remained.

LUGG BRIDGE   *Old Bridge Inn and Parish Church.*

LUGG BRIDGE   *Looking towards English side, Hell Peak in background.*

(To face page 112*).*

LITTLE BRAMPTON FARM   *16th century.*

LITTLE RODD   *16th century and earlier.*

(*To face page* 113).

CECIL PARSONS AND THE RADNORSHIRE COTTAGERS

The hero of this story, Cecil Parsons, was a solicitor and banker, who lived at Stapleton Lodge. A Whig in politics, he was a shrewd business man. He had his enemies, like most strong personalities, and some of the older inhabitants of Presteigne remember hearing stories of his eccentricities from their parents. Nevertheless, he acquired much popularity among many sections of the community for the brave fight he put up on behalf of what were called the Radnorshire Cottagers.

These were the crofters living on the small hillside holdings, which they had reclaimed from the " wastes " and brought into cultivation. There was a widespread belief in Wales, which persisted into modern times, that if a man could erect a dwelling on common land in a night, and have smoke coming from the chimney in the morning, he acquired freehold rights over the land, to the extent of as much as he could enclose in the night with a shallow ditch or wall. When anyone wanted to acquire a holding in this way, friends and neighbours invariably assisted, to ensure his success.

Such houses had the Welsh name of ty-un-nos (house of one night); in Radnorshire they were called, rather aptly, " morning surprises." The custom was claimed to be permitted by the Laws of Howel Dda, who lived 1,000 years ago. The Welsh Land Commission of 1895, although they did not accept Howel Dda, reported that these small enclosures " had played a very considerable part in the actual reclamation and improvement of the higher lands in Wales."

Most of the higher lands in Radnorshire belonged to the Crown, which had not troubled to disturb the crofters. In 1835, however, a large part of these lands was sold, and the wealthy landowners who acquired them, usually at a low price, promptly began to turn out the poor crofters. There were one or two bad incidents, such as turning a sick woman out of bed, pulling her cottage down, and robbing her and her children of all shelter.

Cecil Parsons could take the part of other people as well as his own, and he became the champion of the dispossessed crofters. He lost his case before the Assize Judge at Hereford, and then, at his own expense, appealed to the Court of Common Pleas in London, where Lord Chief Justice Tyndall decided in his favour. The decision had the result of restoring many hundred cottagers to the possession of their small holdings. The new lords of the manors consoled themselves later by extracting rent from the poor people, which seems hardly to their credit. They also got a summons against Cecil Parsons and his friends for "riotous behaviour" attendant on celebrations of the victory, but our solicitor was also equal to that occasion. (There were fireworks and a Guy who, it is to be feared, bore a striking resemblance to a highly respectable magistrate.)

Presteigne left no doubt about its sympathies. When news of the decision was received, the *Hereford Journal* said that " the bells rang merry peals and the information was received by the inhabitants with every demonstration of joy." (The newspapers of those days, by the way, often refer to the Presteigne bells ringing " merry peals " in celebration of some event or other.)

The sequel to the victory was a dinner at the Radnorshire Arms on 20th December, 1837, when the Cottagers' Champion was presented with silver plate subscribed for by over 200 Cottagers. The company included Arthur Wall, of Knill Court, in the chair; Walter Wilkins, M.P., of Maesllwch; the Rev. James Beebee, rector of Presteigne; T. L. Beebee, of Willey Court; Thomas Galliers, of Stapleton ; H. R. Ince, two other parsons, G. Thickens (a leading Baptist), and other prominent Nonconformists.

The large landowners were not there. Perhaps they were not invited. Their absence, in any case, does not appear to have interfered with the merriment of the occasion. The party, numbering more than 70, sat down at 4 p.m., and did not rise until 9.30, by which time, according to the long account which appeared in the *Hereford Journal*, the toast of almost everyone present had been drunk, as well as that of many not present, including lady relatives.

How the Town Took the Castle

As we have already seen, Presteigne castle stood where are now the grounds known as the Warden, and these grounds were presented to the town in 1805 by the fifth Earl of Oxford. At least, this was the town's understanding of the matter, and the grounds had been laid out and used by the town for many years. In fact, until 1870. In that year the town's title to the land was challenged by Lady Langdale, who had succeeded to the family estates on the death of her brother, the sixth and last Earl, in 1853. Lady Langdale let it be known that she had made an arrangement with Sir Harford Brydges, of Boultibrooke, to exchange the Warden for some land belonging to the latter. Lady Langdale's agent, who appears to have instigated the affair, published a notice in the Hereford newspapers to that effect.

Presteigne may be a sleepy place, but its inhabitants are wakeful enough where their interests are concerned, and unapt to let a challenge of this kind pass unnoticed. Moreover, Cecil Parsons was still alive,* and as ready to champion the cause of his fellow

---

* He was then 84, and died at the age of 90 in 1876. There is a tablet to his memory in the chancel of the church.

townsmen as he did that of the cottagers 35 years previously. A public meeting was called, to which Lady Langdale's agent was invited, and came. The meeting's first action was to appoint a committee (consisting of Cecil Parsons, chairman, Captain J. Beavan, J. Davis, R. L. Gawtrey, and J. W. Lewis) for the improvement and maintenance of the Warden. The agent was then allowed to state his case, though he must have felt the battle was already lost. In point of fact, neither side could produce any legal proof of right or wrong. The agent could not disprove the alleged gift, and appeared to base his claims chiefly on the fact that the Earl of Oxford's name had never been removed from the Tithe Schedule, and that the grounds had been neglected for some years. The town could produce nothing in writing to prove the gift, and had to fall back on the evidence of such works as Williams's History, which stated the fact of the gift.

Cecil Parsons and his committee lost no time in entering upon the property, performing several acts of proprietorship, and effecting a marked improvement in its condition and amenities. In doing so they had the sympathy even of the Conservative *Hereford Journal*, which pointed out that unless legal steps were taken to stay their proceedings, "the town's rights were secured beyond all question." The agent evidently withdrew from the contest, for no legal action was taken. . . . And so the castle fell for the last time—into the hands of its rightful owners.

THE BATTLE OF HARLEY HILL

The time came again when Presteigne had to defend its rights. In 1912, a certain gentleman (the builder and first occupant of Silia) took it into his head to erect a fence round Harley Hill and plant trees there for his own benefit. He was quickly reminded that the property he proposed to acquire was part of the ancient waste lands of the Crown Manor of Presteigne, on which the commoners of the said Manor had grazing and other rights, and that the Commoners were not prepared to forgo those rights.

The Commoners found a champion in Mr. R. A. Pugh (still happily a resident of Presteigne), who, despite some local opposition from the friends of the aggressor and threats from solicitors and the like, persisted in his opposition.

At last, one August evening, Mr. Pugh and his friends, who included the Rev. H. L. Kewley, rector, after due notice of their intentions, marched up Harley Hill to remove the fence. They were met at the enclosure by the fencing gentleman and his party, and there the two "armies" faced one another, while their leaders engaged in argument and expostulation. Fisticuffs seemed likely as tempers rose and feelings were unmasked, but order prevailed, and in the end Mr. Pugh proceeded to remove the first staple from a post, with the air and confidence of one laying a foundation stone. This symbolic act completed, Thomas Walters went on with the work, taking down a portion of the posts, fence and all, with a hearty will that did not encourage interference. Might was right in this instance, and the Pugh faction left the field of battle in good cheer, little perturbed by the threats of legal action and dire redress which followed their departure.

Needless to say, they had won a great victory. There was no legal action, and to this day Harley Hill remains unfenced and the Commoners enjoy their ancient rights.

MARY MORGAN

No book on Presteigne would be complete without some account of this poor unfortunate, who was the last of her sex to be hanged publicly at Presteigne. The place where she was hanged is still known as Gallows Lane. It is the lane on the left of the road to Discoed, a short distance beyond the turn for Knighton. The gibbet was standing at the corner for many years, and is remembered by some of the oldest inhabitants.

She was barely 17 years of age, and was hanged in 1805 for the murder of her base-born infant. The father of the infant was a man well known in the county, and he actually sat on the Grand Jury which returned a true bill for murder against the prisoner. It was alleged at the trial that he had incited the girl to get rid of the infant, and had even provided her with an instrument for the purpose. The judge said he should have been standing in her place, but apparently nothing could be proved against him.

The newspapers of the day describe the girl as beautiful, as does the inscription on the tombstone, already referred to in the chapter entitled Parish Gleanings (p. 85). She bore a good character, and was in domestic service somewhere near Presteigne ; if tradition is right, the house was Newcastle Court.

The Judge's final address to the prisoner, before sentencing her to death, was an extraordinary effusion of pious platitude and preachment, without pity or understanding. He was so proud of it that he sent it to his friends and the newspapers.* It is said that he was in tears at the close, but whether at his own eloquence or the prisoner's plight, we cannot tell. That he suffered from remorse afterwards we may believe, since it is on record that he never

---

* It is printed in full in the 1905 edition of Williams's History of Radnorshire.

came to Presteigne again without visiting the grave of Mary Morgan " to revive the impression which she made on his memory." Strangely enough, 11 years later he was taken ill when on circuit at Presteigne, and died there.

A gentleman who was present at the trial, on hearing the sentence of death, immediately took horse for London to ask for a reprieve. In those days condemned prisoners were by law executed two days after their trial, which gave little chance of appeal. In this case a reprieve was obtained, but though he rode through the night, the horseman got back to Presteigne too late to save the prisoner's life.

Public executions never failed to draw large crowds. We wonder whether it would be the same to-day. We may hope not. Pity and horror would surely keep most people away from the execution of a girl of only 17. But it was not so 140 years ago. An old lady of 87, whose grandmother was present at the execution and often talked about it, has told the writer that Broad Street, High Street and Scottleton Street were thronged with spectators when Mary Morgan was taken in the cart from the gaol (then where the Shire Hall now stands) to the place of execution, where a great crowd collected.* The grandmother also said that the girl was unconscious when lifted from the cart, and, as she put it, practically dead before she was hanged. That was a crowning mercy for one who got little from her fellow-creatures.

We to-day can hardly realise the horrors of those early hangings —at which, so clumsily were they done, friends of the victims used to hang on to their legs to hasten death. Parry, in his History of Kington (1845), related of a Kington man who was hanged at Hereford in 1817 that "for about four minutes after the platform dropped he appeared convulsed and frequently exchanged a handkerchief which he held from one hand to another."

AN INTERRUPTED EXECUTION

As has already been told, executions took place in public until 1868. A number were witnessed in front of the gaol on the County School site from the time it was opened (in 1822) up to the 1840's. By that time there were no hangings at Presteigne except for murder—a crime, to give the county its due, which has been of rare occurrence in Radnorshire, at least in the last 200 years. It was

---

* The crowd was probably drawn largely from outside Presteigne. The story handed down to another old resident was that all the houses in Scottleton Street drew their blinds for the occasion, and that if money could have saved Mary Morgan, she could have had "a wagon load ". This resident was told that the girl was put in a winding sheet, from which her hair was seen to hang in long tresses.

during the 1840's that the last execution at Presteigne is believed to have taken place—that of a valet named Harley, who murdered an old man at Knighton for his money.

This little story concerns an earlier execution, in the 1820's or early 1830's. The condemned man was a local farmer; his offence is not known. The morning for the execution had arrived and the usual crowd had assembled to see a fellow-creature suffer. The victim was on the scaffold and the hangman ready, when suddenly a woman pushed her way out of the crowd to the scaffold. It was the condemned man's wife, and even the executioner paused. " Jack," she shouted, " Jack, tell us what field we are to put the potatoes in next year."

The story was told the writer by an old resident, who had it from his grandfather. The latter, who was an eye-witness of the affair, said the answer the woman got had " mighty little to do with potatoes." It sufficiently quelled her not to ask again.

10 DOWNING STREET

There is a tiny 17th century cottage in Green End which, with its garden, forms a triangle, with the road on one side and paths on the other two sides. It stands opposite Paradise Villa. Its own name is Paradise Cottage, but a former occupant dubbed it 10, Downing Street, and as this it is known to-day. There are rumours that our " town improvers " have an eye on this triangle, and thus may disappear another old landmark.

Change, decay, and death are all inevitable. Perhaps an old house, more than anything else, brings this lesson home. The sunny evenings soon pass by, companionships are severed, the hearth no longer cheers—until one day the walls are bare and another tenancy is done.

A past tenant of Paradise Cottage seems to have had some such thoughts, and faced them squarely, for he fixed three tablets to the wall, with verses to convey the lesson. They are in 18th century lettering. The first, which has fallen to the ground and is difficult to decipher, reads as follows : —

This is my paradise of love,
Yet I must go to that above.
When death do call, I must obey,
To quit this place and move away.

The other two verses run less smoothly, and take a more melancholy turn : —

Within this small cottage,
There stands a dart;
That will strike terror
On the proudest heart.

The dart will be gone,
And the shadow fall;
I myself forgot,
Numbered with the dead.

RHYME AND UNREASON.

We seem to have lost our taste for rhymes these days. Perhaps we are more critical than our forefathers, who endured and indeed seem to have liked even the rhyming epitaphs we have already smiled at in this book. It is a pity, though, that the distaste has spread to the children. The radio and the "talkies" they so much enjoy cannot supply the personal touch or evoke the memories handed down from parent to child in the old rhymes repeated by generation after generation. No longer do we hear on Good Friday those lines (not peculiar to Presteigne) :

One a penny poker,
Two a penny tongs,
Three a penny fireirons,
    Hot Cross Buns !

If we can spare these, we should give more cheerfully our pennies for the Guy to those small boys who still bother us on the Fifth of November, to hear them recite the proper rhyme for the day :

Please to remember
The Fifth of November,
Gunpowder treason and plot.
There is no reason
Why gunpowder treason
Should ever be forgot.

Presteigne children used to repeat these rhymes, but their chief occasion was New Year's Day, before 12 of the morning, when, even up to 20 years ago, they came to every house asking for a New Year's gift, and sang for it in a rhyme. There were five pieces in particular which they recited, sing-song fashion, and, as they are rapidly becoming forgotten, they are recorded below, for the satisfaction of the simple, and the possible bewilderment of the " moderns " (who need not read them) :

  I.   Master and missus sit by the fire,
       We poor boys are out in the mire ;
       A penny apiece is our desire,
       Please to give me a New Year's gift.

II.   The cock fled up the yew tree,
      The hen came chuckling by,
      If you hanna' got a ha'penny,
      Please to give me a mince pie.

III. A bowl, a bowl, a bottle of beer,
      Christmas comes but once a year,
      And when it do we'll give you a cheer,
      Please to give me a New Year gift.

IV.   We wish you a Merry Christmas,
      And a happy New Year,
      A pocket full of money,
      And a cellar full of beer,
      A good fat duck and a good fat pig,
      To last you all the year.
      Christmas Box, Christmas Box,
      Please to give me a Christmas Box
          This New Year.

V.   The roads are very dirty,
      My shoes are very thin,
      I've got a little pocket,
      To pop a penny in.
      If you hanna' got a penny
      A ha'penny will do ;
      If you hanna' got a ha'penny,
      Then God bless you.

A DISASTROUS FLOOD

Something has already been said in this book of the plagues of Presteigne, and its great fire. These are in the historical records. The story of the flood is told in the Hereford newspapers of 1838, and is remarkable enough to be added to the town's records. There appears to have been a storm of exceptional violence on 18th June of that year—a real "tempest," as it would be called locally. We are not told what happened to the Lugg, but the storm turned the Clatter Brook into "a considerable river," which, overflowing its banks, swept down Green End, carrying logs and planks from a timber yard there into Broad Street. Here it suddenly emerged with "terrific force," not giving people time even to cross the street out of its way, and for several hours Broad Street was transformed into "a rapid river." By the gaol the flood broke away along the Combe road and carried away the turnpike gate and house near the gaol, from which the gatekeeper was rescued with difficulty. When the flood had subsided, there were holes three or four feet deep in the road. It was perhaps behaviour of this kind which gave the brook its name.

SOCIETIES

The Radnorshire Agricultural Society, which was formed in 1809, originally held its meetings alternately at Penybont and Presteigne. For many years now its shows have taken place at Penybont, but under rather different conditions from the show held there in 1812, when the plough teams might consist of any number of horses *and oxen*. The latter were used at the plough in parts of Radnorshire up to about the 1840's. A writer of 1815 said that "the usual ploughing as well as cart team is composed of two oxen and two horses."

A very different sort of organisation was formed at Presteigne in 1812. This was the Presteigne Association for the Prosecution of Felons, etc.* Its principal object was to put down thieving by the offer of a reward for the arrest of thieves over and above that allowed by Act of Parliament. Its meetings were held at the Radnorshire Arms, D. James was treasurer, and some well-known local gentry of the period were members, including John Harley, H. P. Pyefinch, John and Thomas Galliers, James and Joseph Stephens, and John and Thomas Bodenham. The Bodenham family, by the way, built The Grove about 1770; John, who lived there, had a daughter, who became the mother of Lord James of Hereford.

The Radnorshire Grey Coat Club was a flourishing institution in the 1830's (and later), and met and dined alternately at Presteigne and Rhayader. It was formed in 1835. There are records of meetings at the Castle Inn in 1837 and 1838, with Sir Harford Jones-Brydges in the chair. The Club, according to Mr. Bowen Hamer, was formed to encourage the weaving of home-grown wool into grey cloth. It had a Whig bias and is mentioned in election songs of the period. The members wore grey coats and waistcoats at all Club functions.

SOME WAGE COMPARISONS

Some comparison of the present (1945) local rates of wages with previous years may be of interest. The minimum rate for an agricultural labourer in Radnorshire is 70s. for a week of 52 hours in summer and 48 hours in winter. In July, 1939, the minimum was 33s. a week, and in 1902 married men earned an average of 16s. 10d. a week, including the value of a free cottage and other perquisites. Quarrymen received 16s. or 17s. a week about 1902, and 1s. or 1s. 1d. an hour for a 48-hour week in July, 1939; they now get 1s. 7¾d. per hour, and a production bonus. County Council roadmen got 19s. 6d. a week in 1901, compared with 36s. in July, 1939, and 69s. 6d. at the present time.

---

* An Association with a similar title was formed at Kington in 1821.

NAMES OF THE PAST AND PRESENT

A list of *Deputy Lieutenants* in the sessional rolls of the period around 1835 includes the following in the neighbourhood of Presteigne: The Earl of Oxford, Eywood; Major James Barnes, Presteigne; Sir Harford Jones-Brydges, Bart., Boultibrooke; Lyndon Evelyn, Kinsham Court; Edward Jenkins, M.D., Nantygroes; Peter Rickards Mynors, Evenjobb Court; Richard Price, Norton House; Sir John James Garbett Walsham, Knill Court ; John Whittaker, Newcastle Court.

A *Grand Jury* in 1865 included the following: H. Bridgewater; J. J. Edwards; E. M. Evans; R. Green-Price, M.P. (Norton Manor); E. Jenkins; Sir Harford James Jones-Brydges (Boultibrooke); R. B. R. Mynors; W. T. Mynors; G. H. Phillips; T. Trumper; A. Walsh; Sir John Walsh, Bart. (Knill Court).

The *County Magistrates* who were at the Shire Hall round about 1883 were as follows: Rev. R. L. Venables, Chairman; Rt. Hon. Lord Ormathwaite; R. W. Banks; James Beavan; J. A. Beebee (Womaston); E. Coates (Combe House); W. de Winton; S. C. Evans Williams, M.P.; F. L. Evelyn (Corton); J. W. Gibson-Watt; Sir Richard Green-Price, Bart., M.P. (Norton Manor); R. D. Green-Price (Nantygroes); Sir Harford James Jones-Brydges, Bart. (Boultibrooke); G. A. Haig; Edward Jenkins (The Grove); Rev. Sir Gilbert Frankland Lewis (died 1883); R. B. R. Mynors (Evancoyd Court); T. B. Mynors (Barland); Captain Cecil Otway (Newcastle Court); G. H. Phillips; Rev. W. E. Prickard; C. Coltman Rogers, M.P.; J. P. Severn; General J. R. Sladen; A. G. Vaughan; J. W. Vaughan; Hon. A. H. T. Walsh (Eywood).

The names of the above which are near Presteigne are shown in brackets. It is interesting to note that, of these, only Womaston is still (1944) in the occupation of the same family. After the death of Sir Richard Green-Price in 1887 (the present baronet, Sir Robert, lives at Gwernaffel, Knighton), Norton Manor was bought by Sir Powlett Milbank, Bart., who was M.P. for the county from 1895 to 1900 (and died in 1918); it is now owned by Mrs. Meade. The Grove is now a farmhouse, Eywood is a Girls' School, and Barland a Children's Home. Evancoyd Court is now owned and occupied by the Rev. Claud Lewis, Boultibrooke by L. Otway Clark, Esq.; Nantygroes by R. E. B. Woods, Esq.; Newcastle Court by S. Harold Thompson, Esq. (a former Sheriff of the County); Combe House by General Prescott Decie; and Corton by L. B. Newall, Esq. The Coates and Evelyn families are still represented in the locality—by the Misses Coates at Broad Heath House, and Miss Evelyn at the Vyne.

The Town.—The payments recorded among the Sessional Rolls furnish the names of many of the officials and tradesmen in

the town. The officials of the gaol in 1857 were as follows:—
Governor, Henry Verdon; surgeon, E. M. Tearne; chaplain, Rev.
C. Blackburn. The hall keeper at the Shire Hall was William
Luggar, and the court crier, John Meredith. The county surveyor
was William Wishlade. The tradesmen mentioned in the same
year were as follows: butcher, Samuel Powell; bakers, W. Kitsell,
H. Williams; grocer, Susan Morris; druggist, and grocer, H. Verdon, junr.; ironmonger, E. Newell; shoemaker, E. Cowdell;
printer, H. M. Jones; drapers, Moon and Price; painter and plum-
ber, J. Bush; mason, J. Davies; carpenters, H. Forrester, John
Lloyd, Joseph Price; haulier, F. Hall; corn factor, R. Radnor; coal
merchant, W. Field; blacksmith, A. Johnson.

In 1868 the gaol surgeon was H. K. Debenham, the governor
and chaplain remaining as above. The hall keeper was John
Meredith, and the county surveyor was S. W. Williams. New
names among the tradesmen included grocer, Ann Lloyd; baker,
I. Stedman; draper, James Jones; and tailor, R. Williams.

In 1874 Cecil Parsons was County Treasurer; J. T. Wheeldon,
Chief Constable; T. Callaway, governor of the gaol; W. Stephens,
Clerk of the Peace (a well-known solicitor, who lived at Warden
Court).

In 1879 Samuel Young was hallkeeper, and the tradesmen included: butcher, Ann Powell; grocer, W. Watkins; ironmonger,
E. Newell; printer, H. Martin Jones; draper, W. Hamer; painter,
E. Ince; mason, J. Griffiths; builder, J. Price (W. Cole in 1883);
cabinet maker, J. Vaughan; blacksmith, J. Worthing.

A list of 1894 has the following names: bakers and grocers,
F. Burningham, J. Powell; baker, H. J. Sparey; grocers, Perrott
and Sparey; butcher and dairyman, T. Beavan; butchers and inn-
keepers, G. Harper, M. Howells; butcher, A. Powell; tailors, R. A.
Pugh, W. A. Walters; milliners, etc., A. A. Bufton, Fryzers;
draper and hosier, J. P. Jones; builders, J. Griffiths, J. Price;
plumbers and painters, Cole and Son; painter and picture frame
maker, F. Davis; boot and shoe maker, A. R. Saunders; boot and
shoe stores, H. Kerry; printer and stationer, E. J. Jones; chemist,
A. R. Davies; ironmongers, E. Bufton, J. W. Newell; watch and
clock makers, C. Millichamp, W. T. Williams; saddler, J. Briggs;
blacksmith, J. Smallman; wheelwright, T. Walters; coal merchants,
H. Dingley, J. Morgan; monumental sculptors, Vaughan and Son;
horse and carriage hire, C. Briggs.

At the Horticultural Show of 1912 Lady Brydges was Presi-
dent, and the following were Vice-Presidents: Sir P. Milbank,
Bart., Sir F. Edwards, Bart., M.P., Colonel J. Heap, Major S. N.
Thompson, Rev. H. L. Kewley, Drs. N. Y. Lower, H. K. Deben-

ham and H. A. Debenham; W. H. Banks, C. J. Gwyer, G. W. Green-Price, I. M. Rhodes, C. D. Venables-Llewelyn, E. H. Whitehead. The secretary was G. F. Green, and the auditors, J. Mackintosh and A. M. Thomas. The committee consisted of A. H. Smith (Chairman), W. Beavan, A. Evans, J. J. Griffiths, A. Handley, A. Hicks, H. Mann, W. Palliser, T. Powell, T. D. Pullman, C. Ruff, H. J. Sparey, F. Stalker, W. Thomas, G. S. Tovey, T. Walters, W. T. Woodhouse, W. Wozencroft.

The following were the officials for the Horticultural Show of 1944: Chairman, Rev. C. J. Harding; vice-chairman, O. Gibbin; treasurer, W. E. Davies; secretary, C. Crawford; asst. secretary, H. W. Davies. Mrs. L. B. Newall was Sponsor, and the committee consisted of the following: W. D. Coates, H. H. Constable, Rev. H. B. Curtis, W. Curtis, Mrs. F. Davies, H. A. Davies, Colonel and Mrs. C. B. Evans, Mrs. J. O. Fenton, Mrs. O. Gibbin, Rev. R. I. Gibbs, Mrs. G. F. Green, W. H. Greenhouse, J. E. Hill, E. J. Hitchman, W. H. and Mrs. Howse, Mrs. F. O. Lewis, W. Lewis, J. and Mrs. Mackintosh, T. Perkins, Mrs. W. G. Restall, A. H. Sparey, Mr. and Mrs. G. Taylor, Mr. and Mrs. Griffith Thomas, R. H. Thomas, R. Lane Walker, and Mrs. J. A. Weale.

XIX

From Presthemede To Presteigne

Anyone who has studied old records will know how careless people used to be about the spelling of names. When few people could write, and fewer spell, the scribes employed on documents did the best they could after hearing the names they were required to write. The pronunciation of the names they heard would vary with the individuals concerned, some no doubt being broader or less precise in their talk than others, as happens to-day.

Domesday Book provides an early example. In this case the scribe, who did not understand English, translated the names as he would spell them in his native Norman: thus in Domesday *k* usually becomes *ch*, initial *th* becomes *t* and medial *th* becomes *d*, and the gutturals *h, ch* and *gh* are turned into *st,* and *sh* into *s* or else is prefixed by *e*.

Canon A. T. Bannister, in The Place Names of Herefordshire, gives a further instance in the change which happened to the Saxon termination *worth* (meaning open space, farmlands, etc.). The West Mercian form of this word was " worthign," which in Domesday became " Urdine." Canon Bannister mentions that Strongworth, once Strongwardine, is now Strongwood; also that Lingham, as it was in Domesday, became Lingeyne, and then the present equally meaningless Lingen. These two examples show how dangerous it is to try from the present form of any name to arrive at its original meaning.

The accepted meaning of Presthemede, the original name of Presteigne, has been given in the second chapter of this book. The Rev. Jonathan Williams, in his county history, not looking beyond the present name, pronounced, *ex cathedra* as it were, that the name " is a compound word, of Norman Latin, and is derived from ' Presa,' the fee for depasturing cattle on the royal wastes, and ' Teigni,' officers." Thus, he proceeds, the first inhabitants of Presteigne were " officers appointed to collect and receive the royal revenue arising from the herbage of the forests."

As Canon Bannister points out, mere carelessness was often responsible for changing the form of a name, and instances can be found in any document written before the end of the 18th century. One can find a ready example of this in most parish registers, where the name of the same individual may be spelt differently even on one page. Perhaps some folk who proudly claim some special spelling of their name as a kind of family crest do not realise sufficiently how fortuitously it probably came about, and perhaps, too, how recently.

We are reminded also of the good people who insist on spelling their names with an initial small double *f*. It is true that this form was in general use from the 14th century, but it applied to all *F* names, the reason being that no other form of the capital was known. The habit persisted in some quarters, like the old-fashioned *s* (written as *f*), until after 1800. There was a writer of the Shire Hall records at Presteigne who used the small double *f** up to 1801.

At the present time some spell Presteigne with the final *e* and some without it, and there is argument as to which is the correct form. The Urban District Council itself uses the final *e*, and the County Council also, as do the banks and the motor associations (on their sign posts). The Post Office, Ordnance Survey, and the Great Western Railway, on the other hand, omit the final *e*. Among residents, the majority may be said to prefer to add the *e*.

The same difficulty appears to have occurred in the 13th century—though it probably bothered people less then. In the Charters of Hereford Cathedral, the name was given as Presthemede in 1252; in the Taxatio Ecclesiastica of 1291 (and also the Nonarum Inquisitio of 1341) the name apears as Presthemed. This name persisted until the end of the 14th century, but the Feudal Aids of 1316 introduced a variation, Prestemede, and an Inquisitio post Mortem of 1337 produced a new version in Presthende.

The last marked an important departure, and this rendering formed a basis for other versions for two hundred years, the name being spelt in the same way in a Royal Grant of 1485 and in wills made in 1544 and 1549. It also marked the transition from three syllables to two. Three syllables were still used in 1402 by Edmund Mortimer, who wrote Prestremde, while an Inquisitio post Mortem of the same year used the original name of Presthemede. In 1457 a writer in the Hereford Corporation MSS. spelt the name Presthemde. This is the latest recorded instance of three syllables.

The name continued to include a *d* until about 1550 in some documents. An Act of 1544 spelt it Prestend. Other versions,

---

* Before the 14th century a small single *f* served for the capital. In Welsh, of course, ff is different from f, and the above remarks do not apply in the same way to genuine Welsh names.

taken from various sources, were Presthend (1426 and 1504), Prestheinde (1490 and 1536), Presthunde (1522), Prestende (1540), Presteynd (1548). Note the old difficulty about the final *e* (Presthend and Presthende, Prestend and Prestende). How cleverly this was avoided by Acts made in 1535 and 1547! These actually gave the name as Preston, which seems a pretty good example of what people thought about spelling in those days. A will of 1623 followed suit. Another variation was Prestmede, which is more like the original name, and continued as late as 1544.

An entry in Chancery Proceedings of this last date contains these words: " Presteign otherwise callyd Prestmede." Two rather earlier entries in the Proceedings of 1538-44 gave the name as Presteigne. These are the earliest records of the modern spellings, but some people had evidently begun to use something like the modern pronunciation (Presteen) before this date. The first instance occurs in a will of 1509, where the name is given as Presthene. Bishop Lee had spelt it Presteyne in 1535, and Leland, a little later, Presteine. A document of 1540 spells the name Preesteene, another of 1545, Prestene, and another of 1550, Presttine.

This gives us so far a total of 22 different spellings up to about the year 1550. There are more to come which are set out below. Practically all of them are variations of the modern spellings. These (Presteigne and Presteign) have been the most common forms of the name at all periods since 1550, and the name up to 1750, at any rate, was more usually spelt with an *e* at the end than without it.

The sources of the later spellings are not given in detail. They are for the most part old maps, Government documents of various kinds, wills, and travel books. The dates are shown in each case. A word of explanation seems called for with regard to the *ain* or *ayn* ending which crept in during the 17th century, and perhaps a little earlier.

The worst of the diphthong *ei* is that it may be pronounced (like " either," in fact) with a long *e* or a long *i*. In Hereford Eign Street is pronounced with a long *i*.* The latter sound does not appear ever to have been applied to Presteigne. In its place we have the complication of the long *a*, because in Radnorshire dialect a long *e* tends to become a long *a*. The "reaps" (where neighbours used to meet to cut the wheat) were invariably called " rapes," and a word like " meaning " would be pronounced " maning." There is little doubt, therefore, that Presteigne often got called Prestane.† Thus strangers only hearing

---

* Mr. S. Wright, who has written much about Hereford history, says that this name formerly had an *e* at the end.
† *See* Tailpiece for a modern instance.

the name, when less attention was given to spelling, would spell it to give the long *a* sound. To the Radnorian, *ei* would still convey the sound of *a*. There is an instance of this in the Norton Manor Rolls of 1686, where the word " contain " is spelt " conteign."

Here, then, are the other variations of spelling, in order of the earliest date at which each occurs in the records available:

Presdene	1553	Prestine	1645
Prestinge	1565	Prestigne	1650
Prestaine	1585	Prestain	1676
Prestaigne	1586	Pristeen	1682
Presteygne	1587	Prestean	1695
Prestayne	1610	Presten	1697
Prestayn	1610	Presteiyn	1700
Presteene	1643	Prestein	1790

With the previous list added to the above, the total number of recorded ways of spelling the name becomes 38.

The two early main versions of Presthemede or Prestemede and Presthende, with their many variations, appear to have persisted until the reign of Henry VIII. The present way of spelling and pronouncing the name came into existence during the same reign, and by the end of the reign had practically supplanted the early versions. The spelling has been mutilated from time to time, but the pronunciation has probably remained the same for over 400 years, subject to local peculiarities of speech. For 150 years, the spelling has not varied, except as regards the final *e*.

This brings us to the final question—to *e* or not to *e*. As we have seen, old Acts of Parliament had their own way of spelling the name of the town, and are no guide as to the correct spelling. Even Acts passed since 1800 are inconclusive. An Enclosure Act of 1812 spelt the name Presteigne, but an Enclosure Act of 1813 used the spelling Presteign. As far as antiquity is concerned there is equal authority for both spellings, though in the church registers and other old documents it is more usual to see the name spelt with an *e* at the end than not.

The writer would suggest that in this instance the corporate body of the town should be regarded as an individual. We are all accustomed to spelling (and pronouncing) people's names as they themselves spell (or pronounce) them, and we do so without question or criticism. Therefore, since the Urban District Council spells its own name with the final *e*, that surely should be regarded as the correct spelling. That spelling has accordingly been used throughout this book.

Tailpiece

There is one modern instance of Presteigne being pronounced as Prestane which deserves to be recorded, since it occurs in some well-known verses by Evoe in *Punch*. We may forgive Evoe the poetic licence, for his delightful treatment of the solemn pronouncement by a Bishop of Hereford that there was much " secret cider-drinking " on the border. Evoe concludes with the following stanza, which may well conclude this book:

> But still if strength suffices,
> Before my day is done,
> I'll go and share the vices
> Of Clungerford and Clun,
> And watch the red sun sinking
> Across the March again,
> And join the secret drinking
> Of outlaws at Presteigne.

ROAD MILEAGES FROM PRESTEIGNE

(1) *Places within* 30 *miles.*

Beguildy 15.
Bishop's Castle 20, via Clun.*
Bleddfa 8½.
Brampton Bryan 10, via Lingen.
Builth Wells 22, via New Radnor.*
Church Stretton 27, via Craven Arms.*
Clun 14.
Clyro 18 via Kington and Brilley.*
Craven Arms 19, via Lingen and Leintwardine.
Eardisley 12, via Kington.
Forest Inn (Radnor Forest) 12.
Gladestry 10, via Old Radnor.
Glascwm 16, via Gladestry and Colva.*
Hay 21, via Eardisley and Clifford.*
Hereford 23, via Byton Hand, Stockley Cross, Pembridge, and Watling Street.
Kington 7.
Knighton 7.
Leintwardine 11, via Lingen.
Leominster 14½.
Lingen 6.

Llanbister 17, via Whitton and Llangunllo.*
Llandrindod Wells 21, via Whitton and Penybont.
Ludlow 17, via Lingen and Wigmore.*
Montgomery 29, via Bishop's Castle.
Mortimer's Cross 8.
New Radnor 8, via Beggar's Bush.
Newtown 29, via Knighton and Beguildy*; 32 via Clun and Clun Forest.*
Old Radnor 7.
Painscastle 18, via Gladestry.*
Pembridge 8.
Penybont 15½, via Whitton.*
Rhayader 26, via Whitton and Penybont.
Richard's Castle (ruin), 16, via Mortimer's Cross.
Talgarth 29, via Hay.
Tenbury Wells 20, via Mortimer's Cross.
Weobley 12, via Titley Junction and Lyonshall.
Wigmore 10, via Lingen.

* Indicates longer drives of special interest and beauty.

(2) *Some more distant places.*

London 151, via Beaconsfield, Woodstock, Worcester, and Leominster.

Abergavenny 47, via Hereford.
Aberystwyth 60, via Rhayader.
Brecon 36, via Hay.
Cardiff 78, via Hereford and Abergavenny.
Devil's Bridge 50, via Rhayader.
Gloucester 51, via Leominster.

Llanidloes 40, via Rhayader and Llangurig.
Machynlleth 58, via Beguildy and Newtown.
Monmouth 41, via Hereford.
Ross 37, via Hereford.
Shrewsbury 40, via Craven Arms.
Worcester 42, via Leominster.

Note on Railway Connections.—Presteigne is a terminal station on a branch line of the Great Western Railway from Titley Junction, which is on the line between Leominster and Kington. It is reached from Paddington via Worcester (Shrub Hill) and Leominster, or via Hereford and Leominster.

The nearest L.M.S. station is at Knighton, from where there is a daily bus service to Presteigne. The journey from Euston is made via Stafford (or Crewe) and Shrewsbury. Knighton has direct connections with Swansea and South Wales, and through Shrewsbury, with Lancashire and the North of England. The G.W.R. connects with Shrewsbury through Leominster, and directly with Bristol, Cardiff, etc., through Hereford.

APPENDIX.

Supplement to the Dialect of Radnorshire published in RADNOR OLD
AND NEW (*Jakemans*).

*Since the above was compiled, the writer has authenticated a number
of words etc. omitted from the original list, which are given below for the
benefit of those who are interested in this subject.*

I. *Additional Words.*

afore : common for "before."
banky piece : steep field.
biscake : biscuit.
bron : boar kept for breeding.
brumhook (or brummuck) : short handled bill-hook.
bully head : tadpole.
bundation : abundance.
burnskin : excitable, lively.
burying : funeral.
caddow : may-fly.
case : to case it=to move or run fast.
cex : common for umbelliferous. plants like hogweed, parsley, hemlock.
chaw : wad of tobacco for chewing.
chiwot : marten.
clomber : to climb.
coddlement : a mixture of all sorts ; also "my mind is all a coddle."
comical : queer, unusual ; sometimes bad-tempered or quarrelsome.
corneyweek : lapwing, plover.
create : to give angry words, make a scene or disturbance.
crib : to grumble ; also circular or square feeding trough for cattle.
cubs : specially contrived cupboards in which geese are put to sit.
cues : iron plates formerly put on the feet of cattle driven long distances.
done-ing (dunning) : of a life, drawing to its close.
drashing hook : long-handled bill-hook.
dyche (long y) : dyke, ditch.
eariwig : earwig.
emsin : to do emsin=to make the sign of the Cross.
erra : are there any ? (e.g., "erra letters ? " If none, the answer is "nurran.")
feeding : putting on weight (of men and animals).
fizzles : thistles.

fret : to ferment (often applied to cider).
gurgeons : sharps or "seconds" (after bran) in milling.
hantle : heap, lot (e.g., a hantle of money).
harden : to harden on a person = to drive a bargain, resist an overcharge.
hi-sht (long i) : hush (hisht that noise).
hool : of a pig, to grout.
kag : tear (e.g., made by a nail in clothing) ; also verb, to tear.
keen : to sharpen.
kelp : of a dog, to bark or bay continuously.
kemist : drunk.
Llan Hollan : All Hallows.
lumpin : small pig (say 8-16 weeks).
lunge : to ill-treat (especially animals).
meat : food in general.
mex : to clean out (e.g., a cowhouse).
mimmockin : puny (e.g., a little mimmockin thing).
mis-call : to abuse a person to his face.
moggy : pet name for a calf .
mye : to tread down hay or corn in a store place such as the bay of a barn ; also noun (e.g., make the mye).
nail passer : gimlet.
nettle : to get on with a job (e.g., he's nettling to it).
nobby : a young foal or colt.
noggin : a can, of say 1 or 2 quarts (e.g., a noggin of milk for the calves).
obedience : obeisance (e.g., her did make her bit of obedience=she curtsied).
oddmark : land an outgoing tenant may plough up and sow with wheat.
odds : to move, change (e.g., a farmer to a slow horse, "I'll odds you" ; also, odds your ways).
ort : (of a horse etc. feeding) to put aside waste and select the best.
pendel : perpendicular ; also verb, to rear up (e.g., a ladder).

pentis : the shed attached to a smithy, where the horses are shod.

pinsons : pincers.

plain : without conceit or affectation, straightforward (e.g., she's a very plain lady).

podge : to get stouter (e.g., he do podge uncommon).

pooch : to tread down ground when wet (e.g., cattle in a gateway) ; also poochy=dirty, muddy.

power : a lot (e.g., a power of people).

purgatory : flat piece of perforated iron above the pit of a fire-grate (common with peat fires, which burned for months at a time).

quantityship : quantity.

raisty : rancid.

range : passage in cowhouse near feeding racks (same as the bing).

rattler : the smallest pig of a litter.

rid : to clean in agricultural sense (e.g., land, hedge, etc.)

rise : to get (e.g., to rise potatoes, to rise money at the bank, to rise a railway ticket).

roozel : trans. verb, to keep warm (e.g., of a hen with her chickens) ; also of poultry, to scratch up.

rouk : rut.

rundel : hollow tree, or one badly grown (for timber).

runt : any undersized or underfed-looking animal ; also verb (e.g., them pigs are runted).

scullion gate : lych gate.

shape : portrait (e.g., take my shape, and sometimes, pull my shape) ; also,

coming some shape=to be on the mend from sickness.

snaffle : to take anything on the sly (rather like slang word "scrounge.")

snaggle : to make a bad cut or notch (e.g., in wood).

sniping : sharp, biting (e.g., wind).

spawl : to split off (e.g., wood or stone).

spirtle : to sprinkle, splash.

sprite : lively.

squat (rhymes with cat) : wedge or block with handle, put under a wheel to prevent movement downhill.

squomble : to sprawl, scramble (e.g., over a fence).

steamer : old name for the threshing machine.

stive : to stifle ; stived also=kept in too close a place.

stog : to overeat (e.g., he's fair stogged).

storm : may=very cold weather (e.g., the storm lasted two months).

taber : of a butterfly, to flutter on a window pane.

thrape : to thrash.

torrel : a useless sort of person.

tussicky : of a cough, dry and hacking.

upper warmers : folk from "up country" (the hills) ; sometimes called the uphill folk.

wicked : often applied to children, as meaning lively, restless, playful.

wollies : ridges into which hay is raked before being put into cocks.

woozer : a little pig (up to say 8 weeks).

wozzle : to twist.

wunst : once

yield : to get worse in health.

II. Words previously included.

arf : better spelt as owf.

cabe (or kaib) : also verb, to hoe.

cratch : also (2) rack for hay and straw above manger in stable ; (3) sheep cratch is a feeding trough, usually on wheels.

darchy : better spelt as dakky, but some times pronounced with Welsh ch.

lungeous : also cruel.

middling : also, of health, poorly ; pretty middling often means worse than middling.

niscal : better spelt as nisgul

queek : also a bout of sickness.

quist : also chap, fellow, etc. (e.g., "a queer quist" or "a rum old quist").

romilly : better defined as adj. descriptive of a tangled or confused condition (e.g., a cornfield beaten down by rain, a ravelled skein of wool—both are "a romilly mess").

skelt : also verb, to wander.

suck (sometimes soch, with Welsh ch) : gutter in middle of double cowhouse.

tack : also tools, working kit.

tempest : thunderstorm, rather than mere rainstorm.

III. Welsh words still known in mid-Radnorshire.

ach-y-fi : expression of disgust or dismay (often used by harassed mothers).

mochyn : pig.

tarw (taroo) : bull.

IV. *More typical phrases and expressions.*

There was used to be.
How be you this long time?
The water was froze up all.
He be a very wore-out old man.
He does lep and pop uncommon, he does (said of a lively child; does rhymes with shoes).
Please to come on in.
Please to come on to the fire.
He's gone back up (home again).
He's gone up over (across the fields).
Come bye=get out of the way.
Go bye—go round (e.g., a shepherd to his dog).
Where is he to?—where has he gone?
He do mostly hold towards chapel, he do=he goes to chapel rather than church.
He did lose his one leg=he lost one of his legs.
I dunno did he (or, was he)=I know he did (or was).

I'll come now just=I'll come just now.
It's raining pouring=it's raining very heavily.
He's coming to the fire=he is getting better.
They are more apt to be=they are more usually.
I hope you have it as you like it=I hope you have everything you want.
I know my own know best=I prefer my own way (of doing something).
To have the name of a farm=usually, to be owner in title of a farm which is heavily mortgaged.
To pick a fowl=to pluck it.
As is best=that's a good thing, or, so much the better.
Upon times=now and then.
Reach to=help yourself (at table).
Loose it go=let go of it.
She had a son to die=she lost a son.

INDEX

N.B.—Footnotes are indicated by *n* after page reference.

ADDENDA.

Further research by the writer since this book was compiled has resulted in the following additional information being obtained. Too late for incorporation in the text (since the book is about to go to press), the particulars are given briefly under their appropriate chapter headings, for convenience of reference.

YESTERDAY AND TODAY.

Harford House in Hereford Street belonged to Mr. Harford Jones, the father of the first baronet of that name, who lived at Boultibrook. Mr. Jones sold the house in 1781.

The ground now occupied by the railway station and around it was formerly known as The Burgage. The original name of Back Lane was Further Back Lane, and it was still so called in the early 1800's. Up to that time too (when probably the present house was added) the site now called St. Mary Mill was properly distinguished as St. Mary Mill Barn.

The space around the Church lych gate was called The Scallions. The road at the side of the County School had the name of Broadaxe.

FESTIVAL AND FEAST.

After the calendar was changed in 1752, the date of the Warden Wake was advanced from 24th June to 5th July. Owing to the latter date clashing with the date of the Bishop's Castle fair, it was changed back to 24th June in 1781, but altered to 20th June in 1782, at which date it was to remain " for ever." The fair on 11th December was originally St. Andrew's Fair on 30th November. The other three fairs were started early in the 19th Century.

The Presteigne Race meeting was abandoned about 1851, owing to rowdyism and the number of feuds stirred up between the inhabitants of different localities. It was revived on 5th October, 1864, on the promise of better behaviour in future.

As a sign of the "fashionableness" of Presteigne, it is of interest to note that M. P. Dykes opened a business as peruke maker and hairdresser in 1776, engaging "to fit and make in a manner unknown to the generality of the country trade all sorts of wigs."

Knighton Races were an institution in the 1780's and perhaps earlier. In 1788 they were advertised as taking place on "the new course near Knighton."

WAYFARERS AND INNS.

Another inn has come to light, making our total 27. This was the White Hart, which was evidently of some importance in the 18th century, though closed about the end of that century, and certainly before 1820. It was advertising its own postchaises in 1781, with "good horses and careful drivers to any part of England." The inn was in Hereford Street, and there is little doubt occupied the premises now known as Millfield House, opposite the station approach. These premises had an old brewhouse attached to them, and other signs of having once been an inn.

The Oxford Arms was originally, in the 18th century, in Broad Street, at the house now called Croesaw, two doors above the Shire Hall. This house still has an old brewhouse. The inn was probably moved to its present site in Hereford Street about 1820-30.

The Radnorshire Arms was first opened as an inn in 1792. From later evidence it appears that the Blue Boar was not in Broad Street but in Hereford Street next to the Market Hall, where is now The Farmer's Arms. Up to some time after 1800 the turnpike road to Kington went through Nash, up Trap Hill and near Burnt House, proceeding by way of Rushock and Barton Farms.

PARISH GLEANINGS.

The shed in the western corner of the graveyard occupies the site of the old charnel-house, used as such until about 1850.

INSIDE THE GAOL.

The first policeman (" peeler " as the early police were called) to be appointed for Presteigne in 1857 was murdered under the old larch tree at the top of St. David's Street. His activities against poachers caused deep local resentment, and it is to be feared that not a few were privy to the attack which was made upon him.